Lay Servant Ministries

Guide for Conference and District Committees
2017–2020

Lay Servant Ministries

Guide for Conference and District Committees 2017–2020

Sandy Jackson, Rick Matson, Brian Jackson, Glenna Kyker-Brayton, Diana L. Hynson

Revised by Jodi L. Cataldo

DISCIPLESHIP
RESOURCES

ISBN 978-0-88177-623-2

DR623

Contents

Introduction

Welcome

Welcome to your leadership role in lay servant ministries. This manual is designed to help you serve as an effective conference or district director. Your basic task is to enlist, train, guide, and support lay servants as they equip and prepare others "for the work of ministry, for building up the body of Christ" (Ephesians 4:12).

These guidelines are designed for district and annual conference committees on lay servant ministries. They outline the responsibilities of these roles, describe the categories of lay servant ministries, and identify and describe the components of the lay servant ministries system.

Salt and Light

"You are the salt of the earth. But if salt loses its saltiness, how will it become salty again? It's good for nothing except to be thrown away and trampled under people's feet. You are the light of the world. A city on top of a hill can't be hidden."—Matthew 5:13-14 (CEB)

Each one of us has a responsibility in our spiritual life to be salt and light to others, to help them along on their spiritual journey. Lay servant ministries is one way of equipping laity to be salt and light to the world around them.

As a director of lay servant ministries or a lay servant ministries committee member, you play a key role in the development of disciples by equipping laity to serve in various ministries of leading, caring, and communicating. You are to be salt and light to others who desire to grow in their discipleship.

May God guide your work as you seek to guide and equip others to become salt and light in the world.

For more information or questions, please e-mail Discipleship Ministries at laity@umcdiscipleship.org.

Why Lay Servant Ministries?

In 2012, the General Conference of The United Methodist Church approved legislation to change the name of lay speaking ministries to lay servant ministries. For several quadrennia, various name changes were proposed—none of which adequately described the role of this leadership development program.

Several annual conferences had already changed the name of this ministry in their individual conferences because they believed that many United Methodists were reluctant to become part of a program that required "speaking." The term *servant* was chosen because it best describes what Jesus told his disciples in John 13 after he himself had performed the duties of the lowliest servant.

> After he washed the disciples' feet, he put on his robes and returned to his place at the table. He said to them, "Do you know what I've done for you? You call me 'Teacher' and 'Lord,' and you speak correctly, because I am. If I, your Lord and teacher, have washed your feet, you too

must wash each other's feet. I have given you an example: Just as I have done, you also must do. I assure you, servants aren't greater than their master, nor are those who are sent greater than the one who sent them. Since you know these things, you will be happy if you do them (John 13:12-17, CEB).

The disciples, who were embarrassed by this act of humility, listened as Jesus spelled out the implications of what he had done. He told them what was expected for their own lives. Not only were they to pass on his teachings by word and deed, but they were to do all this through selfless love—by serving one another without pride or prestige.

While there are recognized positions of leadership within communities, our leadership is to follow this model of servanthood. The role of servant that Jesus took (*doulos*) is better translated "slave." In this world, so centered in pride and self, the word *servant/slave* is certainly not a position to be desired. In some cultures, the word means the lowest slave, but we should not be offended. Instead, we should be honored to serve as our Lord and Savior did. Jesus said to the disciples and says to us today, "*Since you know these things, you will be happy if you do them*" (verse 17). The gospel is a life to be *lived*; not just an ideal to be contemplated. We are called to live out our discipleship as servants in leadership.

Our Historical Roots

Lay servant ministries originated in early Methodism. As the Methodist movement grew, there were more society meetings than there were clergy to serve them. John Wesley realized that laity could be effective leaders of these meetings. Laypeople preached, led worship and Bible studies, and visited the sick and the imprisoned. They formed small groups, which were called class meetings, and bands where they were to "watch over one another with love." These early leaders, once known as "exhorters," were the forerunners of today's lay servants.

Early Methodism stressed personal holiness and social holiness. It was, and still is, not enough to be formed in the faith without outward expressions of that faith lived out in homes, workplaces, and communities. The emphasis on an outward expression of faith is stressed through the three tenets of lay servant ministries—*leading, caring,* and *communicating*:

Leading—In lay servant ministries, leadership has many forms. It might include leading Bible studies or other small-group studies, leading mission endeavors globally or within the community, leading in the ministries of the church, and leading in worship settings, and even more.

Lay servants are leaders who can help lead change. One of the changes could be the way ministry planning is done. It is more helpful to look at the things that have gone well than to focus on the failures. Do not get caught up in downward-spiral conversations that lead nowhere except to despair and gloom. Focus and build on the positive aspects. What has gone well? What do you need to do to improve? Try to evaluate all your projects or events using an appreciative inquiry process. (For information on appreciative inquiry, see the resources on pages 83-92.)

Caring—In all they do, lay servants provide a caring presence. They may participate in caring and visitation ministries; welcome strangers and new members; establish ministries that care for the hungry, the naked, and the imprisoned; exhibit care and concern for pastors, staff, and others.

The ministries in which lay servants become involved will depend on the individuals' spiritual gifts and areas of passion. We do not all have the same gifts for mission and ministry, nor are we all passionate about the same things. It is important to discover our spiritual gifts so that our service will be more effective and in line with God's purposes. Spiritual gifts used in the areas for which God has given us a passion will be used effectively.

Communicating—Lay servants respond to the call to share the good news of Christ with others by communicating. Communication might take the form of sharing an encouraging word with those who are suffering, speaking out for the poor and the oppressed, conveying God's Word through preaching, teaching, or speaking in community venues, and living their daily lives as followers of Jesus Christ.

John Wesley believed that every meeting of Methodists should be a time of *holy* or *Christian conferencing*. Lay servants, as leaders, should set the example in each meeting or gathering in which they participate. Our meetings should reflect who we are as Christians, so the format of our meetings will differ from that of a secular meeting.

You will still need an agenda, but that agenda should include time for prayer, a Scripture lesson, and even some singing. Set a spiritual tone for each meeting, and end the meeting with a time of thanksgiving for the work accomplished. If this is God's work, then we should include God in that work.

Undergirding the three tenets of leading, caring, and communicating is spiritual formation. Lay servants are leaders in the church and serve as role models for others. All lay servants, including conference and district directors, must attend to their spiritual growth by practicing spiritual disciplines and participating in an accountability group.

John Wesley knew the importance of being prepared spiritually. He encouraged one of his itinerant preachers in America, "O, begin! Fix some part of every day for private exercises. Whether you like it or no, read and pray daily. It is for your life; there is no other way: else you will be a trifler all your days."("To John Trembath

CORK, August 17, 1760." The Letters of John Wesley. *The Wesley Center Online*, wesley.nnu.edu/john-wesley/the-letters-of-john-wesley/wesleys-letters-1760.) John Wesley himself kept fixed times for daily devotions for more than sixty years; he practiced what he preached. He rose early every day to read Scripture, pray, and write in his journal. He fasted once a week, received Holy Communion as often as possible, attended worship, and practiced works of mercy, such as visiting the sick and those in prison, and caring for the poor. He participated in acts of justice, speaking out against unfair labor practices and unsafe conditions and against the practice of keeping slaves.

What are your spiritual practices? How are you preparing for leadership? Who is "watching over you with love" or keeping you accountable?

Current Mandate

The Book of Discipline (BOD) of The United Methodist Church contains paragraphs that describe lay servants and their function in the churches and the role of lay servant ministries (LSM) on the district and conference level. **This guide is based on the 2016 *Book of Discipline*.**

In the 2016 *Book of Discipline*, oversight for lay servant ministries is named as one of the responsibilities of the General Board of Discipleship (GBOD), which is now called "Discipleship Ministries." The paragraphs that relate to the GBOD describe the agency's role as providing support to conference and district directors of lay servant ministries and to their committees and to the Association of Conference Directors of Lay Servant Ministries. In consultation with conference directors, the GBOD sets standards for certified lay servants, certified lay speakers, and certified lay ministers, and provides teaching resources for use by conference and district committees. Discipleship Ministries has the responsibility of training and enabling the *laos*—the lay members of The United Methodist Church—to enter into mission and ministry and witness.

The 2016 General Conference brought certified lay servants, certified lay speakers, and certified lay ministers under the overarching umbrella of lay servant ministries. In addition, the lay missioner, which has historically been a category of ministry through the National Plan for Hispanic and Latino Ministries, will now become a specialization underneath the category of certified lay minister. This will bring the number of categories to three: certified lay servant, certified lay speaker, and certified lay minister.

(For more information, go to www.umcdiscipleship. org/leadership-resources/ministry-of-the-laity.)

The Missional Nature of Lay Servant Ministries

Mission

The mission of The United Methodist Church is to "make disciples of Jesus Christ for the transformation of the world." The efforts of the lay servant ministries system to help lay servants become equipped to live out their call to mission and ministry must result in outcomes that advance that mission. While we realize that it is God who calls us into faith and discipleship, lay servant ministries can help individuals identify that call. This call to serve is described in *The Book of Discipline,* ¶128: **"all Christians are called to minister *wherever* Christ would have them serve and witness in deeds and words that heal and free."**[1]

The Meaning of Membership

The *Book of Discipline also* states in ¶ 220—*The Call to Ministry of All the Baptized* that "each member of The United Methodist Church is to be a servant of Christ on mission in the local and worldwide community. This servanthood is performed in family life, daily work, recreation and social activities, responsible citizenship, the stewardship of property and accumulated resources, the issues of corporate life, and all attitudes toward other persons. Participation in disciplined groups such as covenant discipleship groups or class meetings is an expected part of personal mission involvement. Each member is called upon to be a witness for Christ in the world, a light and leaven in society, and a reconciler in a culture of conflict. Each member is to identify with the agony and suffering of the world and to radiate and exemplify the Christ of hope."[2]

Outcomes

If we were to ask the pastor of a local church about the fruitful outcomes produced by the lay servants in the congregation, we would expect results to be described as follows: "Because lay servants have been able to respond to their call and have been equipped through the lay servant ministries system, through their ministries and service within and beyond, this congregation has been transformed."

In other words, our *equipping mission* must be focused on *outcomes,* not only in the local congregation that fosters making disciples of Jesus Christ for the transformation of the world but also in the lay servants' roles in the community, workplace, and other areas of daily life.

In other words, our *equipping mission* must be focused on *outcomes,* not only in the local congregation that fosters making disciples of Jesus Christ for the transformation of the world but also in the lay servants'

---

1. *The Book of Discipline of The United Methodist Church–2016.* Copyright © 2016 by The United Methodist Publishing House. Used by permission.
2. Ibid.

roles in the community, workplace, and other areas of daily life.

In the 2009–2012 quadrennium, research was conducted to discover the factors that make local churches "vital congregations." A report called "A Call to Action" describes those contributing factors (www.umc.org/CTA). As a result of that research, our denomination will be focusing the next ten years (or more) on the recommendation to "use the *drivers of vital congregations* as initial areas of attention *for sustained and intense concentration on building effective practices in local churches*" (emphasis added). Lay servants should be at the forefront of making our local churches more vital.

What can we do to make our pastors the best they can be? How can we organize and more effectively lead small groups, Sunday school classes, and youth groups?

Call	Equip	Send
Leading • Caring • Communicating Introduction to Lay Ministry: The BASIC Course • *Discover Your Spiritual Gifts**	*Transforming Evangelism*; God's Mission . . . Our Journey*	Servants who are more outwardly-focused, welcoming, hospitable, invitational and effective in witnessing.
	Called to Preach; From Your Heart to Theirs: Delivering an Effective Sermon; Leading Worship; Planning Worship; Telling Stories; Leading in Prayer; Come to the Table; Come to the Waters; Multimedia Technology in Worship for the Church Volunteer 101; Dancing with Words; Biblical Storytelling; Songs in Worship: United Methodist Hymnody	Servants whose participation in worship services are more enthusiastic and passionate—leading people to encounter Christ and hear a call on their lives.
	Devotional Life in the Wesleyan Tradition; Leading Missional Small Groups; Accountable Discipleship; Class Leaders; Life Together in the United Methodist Connection; Teach Adults; History of the Wesleyan Movement; Lay Servants as Christian Transformational Leaders	Servants who are spiritually deepened people, becoming more Christlike and obeying his call to love God, one another, serve the world, changing lives in the name of Jesus Christ.
	Leading Bible Study; Aging and Ministry in the 21st Century; Lay Pastoral Care Giving; God's Mission . . . Our Journey; Justice in Everyday Life; Lay Servants Lead in Conflict Resolution; Living Our United Methodist Beliefs; Opening Our Doors to All God's Children	Servants with more hands, feet, and hearts serving the community and world in more risk-taking ways. Actively involved in forming disciples of Jesus Christ.
	Afire with God; Justice in Everyday Life; Revolutionizing Christian Stewardship for the 21st Century	More giving and generous servants in terms of time, talent, and treasure to transform the world, near and far. Citizens concerned with and active in measures to preserve God's good creation.

*The *italicized* words are courses (present and future) that are used in the lay servant ministries program.

> ### Key Drivers of Vital Churches
>
> - Effective pastoral leadership, including aspects of management, visioning, and inspiration
> - Multiple small groups and programs for children and youth
> - Mix of traditional and contemporary worship services
> - High percentage of spiritually engaged laity who assume leadership roles

What can we do to enhance existing worship or to organize and conduct additional services in style and content that may help develop vital and fruitful congregations? How can we contribute to the involvement of more laity in leadership roles in the ministry of the church? Opportunities will flow from the answers to these questions and will drive the needs that you and your committee need to fulfill in recruiting, training, and matching your lay servants in ministry and in partnership with churches and clergy throughout your district or conference.

The mission and ministry of each lay servant should be guided by the four focus areas that were adopted by the 2008 General Conference.

As you plan your leadership activities, keep the focus areas in mind so that the best of what United Methodists do is highlighted.

Remember that paragraph 120 of the *Book of Discipline* tells us "the mission of the Church is to make disciples of Jesus Christ for the transformation of the world. Local churches provide the most significant arena through which disciple-making occurs." Lay servant ministries both within the local church and beyond is one of the best systems for disciple making that United Methodists have because it is all about nurture, outreach, and witness through its tenets of leading, caring, and communicating. Any church that engages in an effective program of lay servant ministries will become more vital and fruitful because it equips and empowers the laity for ministry in partnership with the clergy. Such partnership is essential to the fulfillment of the mission of the church.

> ### Four Focus Areas
>
> - Developing principled Christian leaders for the church and the world.
> - Creating new places for new people by starting new congregations and renewing existing ones.
> - Engaging in ministry with the poor.
> - Stamping out killer diseases by improving health globally.

Lay Servant Ministries in the *Book of Discipline*

Lay servant ministries are described in *The Book of Discipline of The United Methodist Church* in *The Local Church*—Section XI, par. 266-269. The categories of ministry under the section on lay servant ministries are certified lay servant, certified lay speaker, certified lay minister, and the National Plan for Hispanic/Latino Ministries (NPHLM) Lay Missioner. To become either a certified lay speaker or a certified lay minister, you must first become a certified lay servant (or the lay missioner equivalent through the NPHLM). *The Book of Discipline* also provides an avenue of equivalency for those within the central conferences. The paragraph for lay missioner moves that category under lay servant ministries as a specialization of a certified lay minister.

Certified Lay Servant

Certified lay servants serve in their local churches and may also serve in the district, the annual conference, and local churches beyond which they hold membership. As disciples of Jesus Christ, lay servants are encouraged to

---

CLASS LEADERS

Class leaders and class meetings were the hallmarks of early Methodism. They were a very effective means of providing nurture and oversight of the members of the Methodist Societies. Class leaders were assigned to watch over those in the class meetings (fifteen to twenty members of the society) with love. They were to see each person in the class once a week to inquire how their souls "prospered" and provide any encouragement or instruction that was needed. Class leaders then met with the minister once a week to inform the minister of any who were sick or in need of spiritual guidance.

---

serve in all areas of their lives. A certified lay servant may also become a class leader with appropriate training. (See the *Lay Servant Ministries Equipping Resources Catalog* for a course on class leaders.)

¶ 266. *Certified Lay Servant*—1. A certified lay servant is a professing member of a local church or charge, or a baptized participant of a recognized United Methodist collegiate ministry or other United Methodist ministry setting, who desires to serve the Church and who knows and is committed to Scripture and the doctrine, heritage, organization, and life of The United Methodist Church and who has received specific training to witness to the Christian faith through spoken communication, to lead within a church and community, and to provide caring ministry.

---

2. The certified lay servant serves the local church or charge (or beyond the local church or charge) in ways in which his or her witness, leadership, and service inspires others to a deeper commitment to Christ and more effective discipleship. The certified lay servant, through continued study and training, should prepare to undertake one or more of the following functions, giving primary attention to service within the local church or charge, United Methodist collegiate ministry, or other United Methodist ministry setting:

  a) Provide leadership, assistance, and support to the program emphases of the church or other United Methodist ministry.

  b) Lead meetings for prayer, training, study, and discussion when requested by the pastor, district superintendent, or committee on Lay Servant Ministries.

  c) Conduct, or assist in conducting, services of worship, preach the Word, or give addresses when requested by the pastor, district superintendent, or committee on Lay Servant Ministries.

  d) Work with appropriate committees and teams which provide congregational and community leadership or foster caring ministries.

  e) Assist in the distribution of the elements of Holy Communion upon request by a pastor.

  f) Teach the Scriptures, doctrine, organization, and ministries of The United Methodist Church.

3. One may be recognized as a certified lay servant by the district or conference committee on Lay Servant Ministries after he or she has:

  a) Obtained recommendation from the pastor and the church council or charge conference of the local church or other United Methodist ministry in which he or she holds membership.

  b) Completed the Lay Servant Ministries BASIC course.

  c) Completed a Lay Servant Ministries advanced course.

  d) Applied to and had qualifications reviewed by the district committee on Lay Servant Ministries, or equivalent structure (See ¶668.3).

4. Recognition as a certified lay servant may be renewed annually by the district committee on Lay Servant Ministries, or equivalent structure, after the certified lay servant has:

  a) Submitted an annual report and renewal application to the charge conference or church council and to the district committee on Lay Servant Ministries, or equivalent structure, giving evidence of satisfactory performance as a certified lay servant. *(See page 64 of this Guide.)*

  b) Obtained recommendation for renewal from the pastor and the church council or charge conference of the local church or other United Methodist ministry in which he or she holds membership.

  c) Completed a Lay Servant Ministries advanced course in the last three years.

5. A certified lay servant may transfer certification to another district or conference upon receipt of a letter from the previous district's committee on Lay Servant Ministries, or equivalent structure, confirming current certification and the completion date of the most recent advanced course taken. Further renewal is in accordance with ¶266.4.

6. It is recommended that a service of commitment be held for persons recognized as certified lay servants.

7. Lay Servant Ministries courses shall be those recommended by the General Board of Discipleship or alternative advanced courses approved by the conference committee on Lay Servant Ministries. Courses should be inclusive of language and cultural groups as relevant to the context. Lay Servant Ministries' courses are open to all, whether or not a participant desires recognition as a certified lay servant.

8. A certified lay servant is a volunteer but an honorarium for pulpit supply is appropriate.[1] *(If an honorarium is received but not wanted, it can be donated to Lay Servant Ministries.)*

---

1. *The Book of Discipline of The United Methodist Church–2016.* Copyright © 2016 by The United Methodist Publishing House. Used by Permission.

Certified Lay Speaker

This category was created at the 2012 session of General Conference to foster excellence, ensure quality, provide accountability, and retain the heritage of laity called to provide pulpit supply. The lay speaker role falls within lay servant ministries; therefore, a lay speaker must first become a certified lay servant. A lay speaker has received specific training to develop skills to serve the church in pulpit supply. While pulpit supply is no more important than other roles within lay servant ministries, it is a valuable and necessary role. Failure to speak with excellence from the pulpit can have deleterious effects on the whole program, and it takes extra effort in developing skills for this role.

¶ 267. *Certified Lay Speaker*—1. A certified lay speaker is a certified lay servant (or equivalent as defined by his or her central conference) whose call has been affirmed by the conference committee on Lay Servant Ministries or equivalent structure to serve the church in pulpit supply in accordance and compliance with ¶341.1.

2. The certified lay speaker serves by preaching the Word when requested by the pastor, district superintendent, or committee on Lay Servant Ministries, in accordance and compliance with ¶341.1.

3. One may be certified as a lay speaker after he or she has:

   a) Been certified as a lay servant (or equivalent as defined by his or her central conference).

   b) Obtained recommendation from the pastor and the church council or charge conference of the local church in which he or she holds membership.

c) Completed a track of study including courses on leading worship, leading prayer, discovering spiritual gifts, preaching, United Methodist heritage and polity, and/or other courses as determined by the conference committee on Lay Servant Ministries or equivalent structure.

d) Interviewed with and obtained recommendation from the district committee on Lay Servant Ministries, or equivalent structure, to be submitted to the conference committee on Lay Servant Ministries, or equivalent structure, for approval and certification.

4. Recognition as a certified lay speaker may be renewed annually by the conference committee on Lay Servant Ministries, or equivalent structure, after the certified lay speaker has:

a) Submitted an annual report and renewal application to the charge conference or church council and to the district committee on Lay Servant Ministries, or equivalent structure, giving evidence of satisfactory performance as a certified lay speaker.

b) Obtained recommendation for continued recognition as a certified lay speaker from the pastor and the church council or charge conference of the local church or other United Methodist ministry in which he or she holds membership.

c) Completed a Lay Servant Ministries advanced course in the last three years.

d) In the last three years, interviewed with and obtained recommendation for renewal as a certified lay speaker from the district committee on Lay Servant Ministries, or equivalent structure, and the approval of the conference committee on Lay Servant Ministries, or equivalent structure for re-certification.

5. A certified lay speaker may transfer certification to another district or conference upon receipt of a letter from the previous district's committee on Lay Servant Ministries, or equivalent structure, confirming current certification and the completion date of the most recent advanced course taken. Further renewal is in accordance with ¶267.4.

6. A certified lay speaker is a volunteer but an honorarium is appropriate.[1] *(If an honorarium is received but not wanted, it can be donated to Lay Servant Ministries.)*

---

1. *The Book of Discipline of The United Methodist Church–2016.* Copyright © 2016 by The United Methodist Publishing House. Used by Permission.

Certified Lay Minister

In 2004, the General Conference of The United Methodist Church approved legislation to form a category of ministry for laity: certified lay minister. Certified lay ministers are people who have received the appropriate training to serve the conference and district as assigned by the district superintendent.

Certified lay ministers (CLMs) may provide pastoral leadership in a small congregation, serve as assistants to the clergy leaders, serve in the pastoral care program, participate in or lead a new church start team, and so forth. Possibilities abound for people in this role. **This is not, however, the next step for all certified lay servants. People serving as certified lay ministers are called to serve intentionally in a specific ministry position.**

There are also specializations available for certified lay ministers that include lay missionary/church planter, United Methodist parish nurse, NPHLM Lay Missioner, children's faith formation, men's ministry, pastoral ministry, and more. For more information, visit www.umcdiscipleship.org/leadership-resources/ministry-of-the-laity.

¶ 268. *Certified Lay Minister*—1. A certified lay minister is a certified lay servant, certified lay missioner, or equivalent as defined by his or her central conference, who is called and equipped to conduct public worship, care for the congregation, assist in program leadership, develop new and existing faith communities, preach the Word, lead small groups, or establish community outreach ministries as part of a ministry team with the supervision and support of a clergyperson. A certified lay minister is assigned by a district superintendent in accordance with ¶419.2.

2. The certified lay minister serves to enhance the quality of ministry much like a class leader did in early Methodism through service in the local church, circuit or cooperative parish, or by expanding team ministry in other churches and charges. As with lay ministry in early Methodism, the certified lay minister uses his or her spiritual gifts as evidence of God's grace.

3. One may be recognized by the conference committee on Lay Servant Ministries, or equivalent structure, as a certified lay minister after he or she has:

   a) been certified as a lay servant, lay missioner, or equivalent as defined by his or her central conference;

   b) obtained written recommendation from the pastor and the church council or charge conference of the local church in which he or she holds membership;

   c) completed a track of study for certified lay ministers relevant to the candidate's assignment as defined by the General Board of Discipleship, or the National Plan for Hispanic/Latino Ministry in collaboration with the General Board of Discipleship, and the conference committee on Lay Servant Ministries or equivalent structure;

   d) Received a letter of recommendation from his/her district superintendent;

   e) Had all requirements for certification, including appropriate screening and assessment as defined by the annual conference, reviewed by the conference committee on Lay Servant Ministries, or equivalent structure, for referral to the district committee on ordained ministry for examination of persons who have applied in writing to be certified lay ministers and to make recommendation for certification (see ¶666.10). After the district committee on ordained ministry interviews the candidate, the district committee on ordained ministry will make a recommendation to the conference committee on Lay Servant Ministries for final certification by that committee.

4. Recognition as a certified lay minister may be renewed every two years by the conference committee on Lay Servant Ministries, or equivalent structure, after the certified lay minister has:

a) submitted an annual report to the charge conference or church council where membership is held and to the conference committee on Lay Servant Ministries, or equivalent structure, giving evidence of satisfactory performance as a certified lay minister.

b) obtained a ministry review by the committee on pastor-parish relations, church council, or charge conference from the congregation of which he or she is a member, or when under assignment, from the committee on pastor-parish relations, charge conference, or supervisory board of the ministry setting in which he or she is assigned;

c) completed a Lay Servant Ministries advanced course or approved continuing education event, as defined by the conference committee on Lay Servant Ministries or equivalent structure in the last two years;

d) obtained recommendation for recertification from the district superintendent;

e) had all requirements for recertification reviewed by the conference committee on Lay Servant Ministries, or equivalent structure, for referral to the district committee on ordained ministry for examination of persons who have applied in writing to be renewed as certified lay ministers and to make recommendation for recertification (see ¶666.10). After the district committee on ordained ministry interviews the certified lay minister, the district committee on ordained ministry will make a recommendation to the conference committee on Lay Servant Ministries for final recertification by that committee.

5. A certified lay minister may transfer certification to another district or conference upon receipt of a letter from the previous conference committee on Lay Servant Ministries, or equivalent structure, confirming current certification and the completion date of the most recent advanced course taken. Further renewal is in accordance with 268.4.

6. A certified lay minister is not eligible for support by equitable compensation funds or pension funds that are provided for clergy. If a certified lay minister is a lay staff member of a church, circuit or cooperative parish, the local congregation is encouraged to provide compensation and withhold taxes appropriate to a layperson.[1]

1. *The Book of Discipline of The United Methodist Church–2016.* Copyright © 2016 by The United Methodist Publishing House. Used by Permission.

Lay Missioner

The National Plan for Hispanic and Latino Ministries (NPHLM) has partnered with the certified lay ministry (CLM) program and will use the same process as the certified lay ministry program. The CLM Modules I-IV in the Spanish language being developed by the NPHLM will cover the same content as the modules provided in the English language. For those seeking a certificate of recognition as a CLM with specialization as a NPHLM Lay Missioner, that certificate will be provided by the NPHLM after completion of the requirements set forth on the CLM specialization infosheet. All former/current lay missioners are required to complete the CLM process to retain status as a lay missioner.

¶ 269. *Lay Missioner*–Lay missioners are committed laypersons, mostly volunteers, who are willing to be trained and to work together as a ministry team with their pastor-mentor, in order to develop and lead faith communities, establish community ministries, develop church school extension programs, and engage in congregational development with and into the local community. Lay missioners are formed according to, and follow the guidelines established by, the National Committee of the National Plan for Hispanic/Latino Ministry, working in conjunction with the annual conference. They are certified jointly by their annual conference and the National Plan for Hispanic/Latino Ministry. The ministry team is supported by and accountable to the local congregation, district or annual conference entity that assigns it to its mission. The concept of the lay missioner is based theologically on the ministry of the laity, in order to complement the work of the pastor.

A certified lay missioner shall be equivalent to a certified lay servant in the processes of certification as a lay minister (¶ 268.3-6); and the Module I-Module II formational sequence and Module IIIs for continuing education of the National Plan for Hispanic/Latino Ministry shall be equivalent to the track of study for certified lay ministers relevant to the candidate's assignment, and the advance course or approved continuing education events described therein.[1]

---

1. *The Book of Discipline of The United Methodist Church–2016.* Copyright © 2016 by The United Methodist Publishing House. Used by Permission.

Position Descriptions

Conference Director of Lay Servant Ministries

The position of conference director of lay servant ministries (LSM) is to be filled in a manner to be determined by the annual conference. **This position shall be filled by a certified lay servant** (BOD, par. 631.6.d.). The conference director of lay servant ministries chairs the conference committee on lay servant ministries or its equivalent, is a member of the conference board of laity (BOD, par. 631.3), and is a lay member of the annual conference (BOD, par. 32). As the conference director of lay servant ministries is a lay member of the annual conference, he/she should make every effort to attend the annual conference sessions.

A conference director of lay servant ministries is a person who has experience in lay servant ministries within the local church and district. This person is aware of the responsibilities of this position and must be open to opportunities for lay servants to serve in various capacities and be able to develop cooperative relationships. A conference director of lay servant ministries provides direction both spiritually and procedurally to the conference committee on lay servant ministries and the conference board of laity.

The conference director of lay servant ministries works with the district directors of lay servant ministries to provide support and direction for the development of laity training within the districts. The conference director may also work with district superintendents in finding suitable candidates for the position of district director of lay servant ministries.

An effective conference director of lay servant ministries works with the conference lay leader, the district directors of lay servant ministries, the conference committee on lay servant ministries, and the conference board of laity to equip the laity of the annual conference for mission and ministry by providing a system for developing principled Christian leaders so that the mission of the church—to make disciples of Jesus Christ for the transformation of the world—is fulfilled. An effective conference director of lay servant ministries also sees lay servant ministries as a vital part of a larger discipleship system in the annual conference, the districts, and the local churches.

QUALIFICATIONS

Spiritual gifts:

- Encouragement (exhortation)
- Leadership
- Wisdom
- Discernment
- Apostleship
- Administration
- Shepherding
- Teaching

Experience and Skills:

- Certified lay servant
- Leadership at the district level (preferably a member of the district committee on lay servant ministries)

- Ability to communicate effectively
- Good listening skills
- Organizational skills
- Ability to share vision, set goals, and monitor progress

RESPONSIBILITIES

- Commit to support the laity (lay servants and others) in spiritual formation and development of skills in leading, caring, communicating and discipleship to help grow vital congregations and increase missional presence in the community
- Train district directors of lay servant ministries in their roles
- Interpret the needs of the annual conference for training opportunities
- In conjunction with the district superintendents, recruit qualified district directors
- Support district directors as they provide training opportunities for all laity
- Be alert to opportunities in which lay servants can serve and lead in mission
- Nurture and support lay servants in their various roles
- Keep accurate records of certified lay servants, certified lay speakers, and certified lay ministers within the conference
- Train district directors to keep accurate records of certified lay servants, certified lay speakers, and certified lay ministers within their districts
- Provide forms of recognition for certified lay servants, certified lay speakers, and certified lay ministers
- Become a member of the Association of Conference Directors of Lay Servant Ministries
- Chair the conference committee on lay servant ministries or its equivalent
- Establish/maintain budget line of lay servant ministries items, if appropriate
- Be cognizant of income/expenses
- Make sure district directors know they can come to conference directors for resources

Conference Committee on Lay Servant Ministries

Every annual conference is encouraged to create a conference committee on lay servant ministries or equivalent structure to fulfill the requirements of paragraphs 266-269 in the *Book of Discipline* and to relate to the conference board of laity and the General Board of Discipleship as per paragraph 1116 and others that might apply (BOD, par. 631.6.a).

The purpose of a conference committee on lay servant ministries is to set criteria and guidelines for district committees on lay servant ministries, develop lay servant courses and approve courses developed by district committees, and organize conference-wide lay servant events (BOD, ¶ 631.6.b.).

The members of this committee at minimum are the district directors of lay servant ministries or their equivalent. Officers may be elected by the committee as it deems necessary. The conference director of of lay servant ministries serves as the chair. (BOD, par. 631.6.c. and par. 631.6.d.).

RESPONSIBILITIES

- Relate to the conference board of laity and the General Board of Discipleship (Discipleship Ministries)
- Set criteria and guidelines for district committees on lay servant ministries
- Using the criteria established, the General Board of Discipleship (Discipleship Ministries) and the education committee of the Association of Conference Directors of Lay Servant Ministries:
    a. develop courses to fill a specific need within the annual conference and that are not available from Discipleship Ministries
    b. approve courses developed by district committees
    c. approve alternative advanced courses (including online courses) that meet the criteria for a lay servant ministries course

- Organize conference-wide lay servant ministries events
- Cooperate or partner with districts in conducting district events
- Train district directors to keep accurate records within their districts (see *Administrative Tasks and Recordkeeping* on page 35)
- Provide track of study to cover CLM Modules I-IV in consultation with the General Board of Discipleship
- Provide oversight of CLM process and appropriate recordkeeping
- Approve the recommendations for certification and recertification of lay speakers and lay ministers by their respective district committees

To help you assess the work of your committee, use the worksheets that are available in the Appendix.

District Director of Lay Servant Ministries

The position of district director of lay servant ministries (LSM) is to be filled in a manner to be determined by the district. **This position shall be filled by a certified lay servant** (BOD, ¶668). The district director of lay servant ministries chairs the district committee on lay servant ministries, or its equivalent, is a member of the district board of laity (BOD, ¶ 667.2), and is a member of the conference committee on lay servant ministries (BOD, ¶ 631.6.c).

A district director of lay servant ministries is the front-line leader for this important system of leadership development within the local church and district. This person is aware of the responsibilities of this position and must be open to opportunities for lay servants to serve in various capacities and be able to develop cooperative relationships. A district director of lay servant ministries provides direction both spiritually and procedurally to the district committee on lay servant ministries and the district board of laity.

The district director of lay servant ministries works with the conference director of lay servant ministries to provide support and direction for the development of laity training within the districts. The district director may also work with the district superintendent in finding suitable candidates for lay servant ministries instructors and members of the district committee on lay servant ministries.

An effective district director of lay servant ministries works with the district lay leader, the district superintendent, the district committee on lay servant ministries, and the district board of laity to equip the laity of the district for mission and ministry by providing a system for developing principled Christian leaders so that the mission of the church—to make disciples of Jesus Christ for the transformation of the world—is fulfilled. An effective district director of lay servant ministries also sees lay servant ministries as a vital part of a larger discipleship system in the local churches of the district.

QUALIFICATIONS

Spiritual gifts:

- Encouragement (exhortation)
- Leadership
- Wisdom
- Discernment
- Apostleship
- Administration
- Shepherding
- Teaching

Experience and Skills:

- Certified lay servant
- Leadership at the district level (preferably a member of the district committee on LSM)
- Ability to communicate effectively
- Good listening skills
- Organizational skills
- Ability to share vision, set goals, and monitor progress

RESPONSIBILITIES

- Commit to support the laity (lay servants and others) in spiritual formation and development of skills in leading, caring, communicating, and discipleship to help grow vital congregations and increase missional presence in the community

- Interpret the needs of the district for training opportunities
- Recruit qualified course instructors
- Be alert to opportunities in which lay servants can serve
- Nurture and support lay servants in their roles and responsibilities
- Keep accurate records of lay servants within the district and help local church leaders to do this within their congregations
- Provide for forms of recognition for certified lay servants, certified lay speakers, and certified lay ministers
- Keep training opportunities open to **all laity**
- Chair the district committee on lay servant ministries

District Committee on Lay Servant Ministries

The district committee on lay servant ministries relates to the annual conference through the conference committee on lay servant ministries. It is chaired by the district director of lay servant ministries. Membership includes the district lay leader, the district superintendent, an instructor of lay servant courses, and other resource people as needed (BOD, ¶ 668.2). The purpose of this committee is to plan and supervise the program within the district.

Responsibilities

- Provide basic and advanced courses for lay servants as recommended by Discipleship Ministries, or as approved by the conference committee on lay servant ministries
- Decide who will be recognized as certified lay servants
- Interview, review records, and recommend for approval by the conference committee on lay servant ministries certified lay servants who have completed the requirements to become certified as lay speakers
- Help match certified lay servants, certified lay speakers, and certified lay ministers with service opportunities
- Support and affirm lay servants, lay speakers, and lay ministers as they serve
- Plan advanced courses for lay servants that will enable certified lay servants and certified lay speakers to maintain that recognition
- Report to the pastor and charge conference of each certified lay servant and certified lay speaker the courses that have been satisfactorily completed by the certified lay servant and certified lay speaker

To help you assess the work of your committee, use the worksheets available in the Appendix of this guide.

Leading the Lay Servant Ministries System

Introduction

Because the mission of The United Methodist Church (and, therefore, its lay servant ministries program) is to "make disciples of Jesus Christ for the transformation of the world," our vision as leaders must take us there. As stated earlier, we envision a laity "equipped to live out their call to mission and ministry." We envision United Methodist laity equipped for all facets of lay ministry that work to make the local church vital and fruitful and to extend the mission of Jesus Christ into the world. As leaders, we need to keep a missional vision at the forefront of our process of calling, equipping, and sending our lay servants.

Both leadership and management are required for successful lay servant ministries. Leaders have a distinct role. They cast a vision, align people and resources to the vision, and motivate stakeholders to fulfill the vision. We have a "missional" vision provided under the Lordship of Christ. We are called to do the hard work of communication to align our district and conference stakeholders in fulfilling the mission. And by keeping the natural rewards and consequences in front of everyone, we motivate and inspire laity, clergy, lay servants, pastors, teachers, caregivers, all to the achievement of the mission for the sake of Christ.

Our conference and district committees are called to

Managers:

- Plan
- Organize
- Coordinate
- Direct

manage the process. We plan, organize, coordinate, and direct. An orchestra is a good metaphor. The music could never be played without the guidance of the conductor and his ability to bring all the elements together into one harmonious

Leaders:

- Provide Vision
- Align People
- Motivate and Inspire

John Kotter, *Force for Change.* The Free Press, 1990, page 5.

whole. Be intentional in ensuring that all the elements—planning, organizing, coordinating, and directing—are included in your management process.

Spiritual Formation

Spiritual formation should permeate the lay servant ministries program. Be intentional in nurturing the faith development of lay servants (and conference directors and district directors). Every course is an opportunity for spiritual formation. The devotion at the beginning of each session is designed to set a spiritual tone for the course. Intentional faith development is essential to the motivation and ministry of lay servants. *Devotional Life in the Wesleyan Tradition* is a course that can help develop intentional spiritual growth. Lay servants should be steeped in spiritual formation. It would be an important topic for a committee weekend retreat.

Components of the Lay Servant Ministries System:

- Spiritual Formation
- Recruiting (Calling)
- Equipping
- Sending

Another means of spiritual formation may be to form lay servant clusters—possibly accountability groups—by phone or electronic means if distance is a problem. Today, there are a variety of ways to communicate—social networking, SKYPE, and so on. Lay servants should also be encouraged to lead or participate in spiritual development activities within their congregations.

Recruiting (Calling)

When asked how her lay servants were doing, one pastor responded, "Oh, if anything is to get done in my congregation, it is the lay servants who do it." Every congregation should have a group of mutually supporting lay servants. Where do you find them? Your lay servants should be recruiting them within their own congregations. In every advanced course, have the facilitator take a few minutes to talk about recruitment. Provide brochures so facilitators have a tool for recruitment. Make sure lay servants understand the history and the scope of lay servant ministries so that they will be effective recruiters for the program.

> In every advanced class, have the facilitator take a few minutes to talk about recruitment.

EQUIPPING

Ensure that your training programs are of such quality that they are highly recommended to everyone, including those who are not currently lay servants. Work with the clergy so that they have the same understanding of the history and breadth and the same tools. If you have eighty churches in your district, you ought to have more than eighty lay servants. And there should be lay servants in each congregation to cover a variety of gifts and services. Ask the district superintendent to give you five minutes at his/her next clergy gathering. Ask one of the clergy who effectively uses lay servants to be a supportive witness at that gathering. Be intentional. Be prepared to explain that lay servant ministries is not just about speaking or preaching. Emphasize that anyone can take one of the courses without being or becoming a lay servant.

Lay servant ministries courses may also be used in other venues, such as the local church, for equipping the laity to answer their call to mission and ministry. Lay servant ministries courses are an excellent component of any discipleship system. To make disciples of Jesus Christ for the transformation of the world, it must be the vision of lay servant ministries to see United Methodists equipped for all facets of lay ministry. You and your team are responsible for bringing that vision to fruition.

Course Selection

Courses must first meet the needs of local churches in their disciple-making mission, and they must meet minimum standards and criteria to be recognized as lay servant courses. A catalog of approved courses is available for viewing and downloading from the Upper Room Bookstore at bookstore.upperroom.org or at www.umcdiscipleship.org/leadership-resources/ministry-of-the-laity.

To order a printed catalog, call 1-800-972-0433 and ask for Item # M184. Courses listed in the catalog include the Introduction to Lay Ministry: The BASIC Course, advanced courses, and a variety of approved online courses through BeADisciple.com. All approved advanced courses meet the requirements for lay servant certification.

Basic Course. The *Introduction to Lay Ministries: The Basic Course* and *Leader's Guide* provide the foundation for lay servant ministries training and meet the course requirements of the *Book of Discipline*. The course addresses the call of all believers, the Wesleyan emphases of United Methodism, and the equipping of laity for the roles of leading, caring, and communicating. It is an excellent primer and could be employed by lay servants to teach members in local churches. It is also readily adaptable as a youth basic course. The course has a ten-hour requirement that can be accomplished with ten hours of classroom contact, with a hybrid model, or with eight hours of classroom contact and two hours of outside preparation that might include reading of the text and a one-page reflection paper on the text. There are no plans to offer the Basic Course online because it was specifically designed around a personal small-group setting so that participants receive formation and grounding to live life as lay servants.

Advanced Courses. Advanced courses are at the heart of equipping people for mission and ministry, and lay servants should be encouraged to participate as often as possible. That means your offerings need to be done with excellence. Courses may be selected from the approved list in the *Lay Servant Ministries Equipping Resources Catalog*, developed locally, or be approved events that meet the needs and requirements of lay servant ministries. Courses developed locally must be approved by the conference committee on lay servant ministries and must meet the requirements of ten hours, applicability to lay servant ministries, include the reading of an assigned text, and lead to opportunities for service in mission and ministry.

> The minimum standard of the ACDLSM for all advanced courses is ten hours.

Alternative Advanced Courses (Exception Credit). Occasionally, there are events or seminars that may meet the criteria for an advanced course in lay servant ministries. See the suggested criteria below.

An approved alternative advanced course is expected to:

- Include readings (Bible, textbook, and other materials)
- Include class discussion and exercises

- Be descriptive (who and what), analytical (figuring out how), theoretical (explaining why)
- Be practical (showing how-to and allowing practice, observation and/or demonstration)
- Provide resources so class members have something to take back and go further with; e.g., reading list(s), websites, general church resources, information about other organizations' newsletters, publications, events, memberships
- Include an assignment to be done outside of class time, either before or after (follow-up to verify completion of post-class assignment may be done by the district committee, if not by the instructor)
- Include an evaluation of completed assignments

Alternative Avenues for Training. Technology is allowing alternate avenues for training either in web-conference settings, online, or in combination of online and face to face. Conferences have adapted some approved courses to be taught online. Beadisciple.com has a number of online courses that have been recommended as meeting the criteria for an advanced course. Web-conferencing allows a course to be taught at one area of a district or conference and streamed to another. Certification of lay servants falls to the district committees, and lay servants should be directed to their committee before relying on an online course hosted by another venue for recertification. Equipping through these means of training should be encouraged while balanced with community-building that can occur with face-to-face courses within the districts. Be creative and equipping.

Course Facilitator Selection

Facilitators can make the course–both in terms of quality and expertise. Whenever possible, co-facilitating can bring expertise and a dynamic to a group that a single facilitator cannot. Look for facilitators (and co-facilitators) with experience, training skills, an appreciation for and support of lay servant ministries, and a love of Jesus Christ. Often, clergy and laity make effective teams and serve as a model for lay–clergy partnership. The district superintendent can be relied upon to recommend teaching pastors with course expertise. Your churches may have subject matter experts. Some course facilitators might also be local college teachers, chaplains, deaconesses or home missioners, or other laypersons gifted in course facilitation. Conferences are encouraged to provide training for facilitators. (See *Training the Trainers* on page 47.)

Because you want to take advantage of the gifts and graces of the facilitators you select, setting broad expectations provides them the opportunity to do their best. But expectations must be set. It is part of the director's task of delegation. So be sure to set goals and competency standards. A suggested format is presented here. Although flexibility is sought, these five elements need to be explicit:

- **Desired results** (Not methods). Identify what is to be done and when. What should the outcome be? We are teaching the course "so that . . ."
- **Guidelines.** Specify the parameters (policies, principles, use or the development of the leader guide, etc.) within which the results are to be accomplished. You may include what works and what does not.

For every planning element, ask:

- **Who**: Leaders, Teachers, Recruiters, Students, etc.
- **What**: Needs, Topics, Basic, Advanced, Languages, Resources, Texts, Meals, Worship, Music, Hospitality, Publicity, etc.
- **When**: Calendar Coordination, Seasonal Impact, Backward Planning (of all activities), etc.
- **Where**: Access, Venue, Recent Classes, Availability, Online, etc.
- **Why**: Needs, Frequency, Opportunity, etc.
- **How**: Guidelines, Format, Technology,
- **How Much**: Cost Estimate, Funding Sources, Tax Exemptions, etc.

- **Resources.** The human, financial, technical, or organizational support available (and what may not be available and therefore what the teacher may need to develop) to accomplish the desired results.
- **Accountability.** Set up the standards of performance and how they will be evaluated.
- **Consequences.** Determine consequences—good and bad, natural and logical—as a result of accomplishing or failing to accomplish the desired results.

(Adapted from Stephen Covey, *7 Habits of Highly Effective People,* Simon & Schuster, 223)

Planning for Training

Planning is critical in managing your system. Without a plan, there can be no effective organizing or coordination. Do not plan alone. Use your committee on lay servant ministries to assist you. At the district level, the committee should consist of the director, district superintendent, district lay leader, and an instructor of lay servant courses—at a minimum. Laity and pastors who are excellent teachers and passionate about the program may also be added. Make sure a variety of gifts are included, such as hospitality. Use the checklist in the *Appendix* of this book to model your activities.

Scheduling. Most approved courses are broken into five sessions, providing a break between each session. This allows time for outside reading and preparation and to digest subject matter. Total length of courses is a minimum of ten hours (some conferences add additional suitable content). Multiple sessions also allow the opportunity for collaboration and for building friendships and associations within the lay servant community. Several formats are possible:

- Two five- to six-hour sessions on Saturdays or a Saturday/Sunday combination with one to three weeks between.
- A weekend retreat beginning Friday evening and extending into Saturday and/or Sunday; time

should be made available for both spiritual formation, reflection, and preparation within the framework. **Providing advance notification to participants regarding assignments and preparation to be done before the weekend is essential in this format.**

- Five weekday or evening two-hour sessions (five successive Sunday afternoons is another alternative).
- Ten one-hour sessions over a period of ten weeks in a small-group setting.
- A combination of online and face-to-face settings (hybrid).
- Eight-hour session on a Saturday with two hours of homework including a one-page reflection paper on the participant's text.
- Online studies (available through www.beadisciple.com).

If you or an appropriate person in your district or conference would like to facilitate an online course, *BeADisciple.com* offers training in the basics of planning, teaching online workshops, and using their Blackboard software. Not all of the courses at *BeADisciple.com* are pre-approved as lay servant ministry courses. Those that are approved by Discipleship Ministries and the Education Committee of ACDLSM are marked specifically as *Learning & Leading* courses. Conferences are encouraged to review the online studies offered and determine if they will give credit to their participants. The recommended standards are that a course should focus on at least one of the basic tenets of lay servant ministries—leading, caring, communicating, and spiritual formation.

Publicity. Publicity is important for recruiting and program success. Your event must be planned in a timely manner. Planning should allow flyers and registration forms to be distributed or posted online a minimum of forty-five days—and preferably sixty days—prior to the event. The calendar should be set three to six months in advance and an e-mail "save the date" notice distributed widely.

- Send save-the-date information three to six months before the event.
- Distribute flyers forty-five days before the event.
- Send a reminder two to three weeks before the event.

Publicity is only as good as the message received and absorbed. In our busy lives, it is recommended that publicity be sent at three different times by three different media (mail, e-mail, newsletter, newspaper, net-news, social network, church bulletin, etc.) **Remember that not everyone has electronic means of communication.** If you ask churches to advertise, prepare a "cut and paste" announcement for bulletins and newsletters and provide flyers for bulletin boards and website postings. Ask lay servants in churches to stand and make announcements during the worship service.

Hospitality. Christians are in the hospitality business. Hospitality puts people at ease and is a model for their future roles. It is easy for a busy director or teacher to get caught up in the details of class preparation and not make himself or herself available for the arriving students. It may be best to have a hospitality person available to ensure that people are welcomed and that there are no surprises. **Not all have the gift of hospitality. If you do not, make sure to recruit someone who does.**

Ideas for effective hospitality:

- A letter or an e-mail setting out expectations and providing good directions.
- Signs on the day of the course (especially with large facilities, there should be signs in the parking lot that lead participants into the classroom.)
- Accessibility
- Refreshments (Consider the variety of dietary needs and refreshment tastes. Not all drink coffee black and not all drink coffee. Consider including fruit or other healthy foods. Hospitality is not free. Make sure that you have taken the costs into account.)

- Registration (A convenient setup to complete the registration process should be included.)
- Spiritual hospitality (The opening, closing, music, worship, consecration of lay servants is all part of sending the participants forth with Christ in their hearts and equipped for the mission/ministry at hand. A commitment service for lay servants is available in *The United Methodist Book of Worship*.)

(See Lay Servant Ministries Training Checklist in the *Appendix*; also available for download at www.umc-discipleship.org/laity under Lay Servant Ministries Resources.)

Planning for Take-Aways. Every course should be planned with a concrete result in mind. What do you want the participants to do following the course? What is their plan for doing it? These are part of the "sending" process. Too many classes are great experiences with no plan for follow up. What should the students have in their hands when they leave? What is their task, their first step? What will they do, or whom will they see first? Suggesting that they should talk to their pastors *before* the course sets up a conversation with the pastors for ministry within the church *following* the course. You may have the opportunity to create a website or social network that will allow students to report on their actions following the course. One district calls for a report from the students three months following the completion of the course as part of the course requirement. How will you assure that accountability is part of your lay servant ministries system?

Take a few minutes in each course introduction to encourage participants to glean ways that can be taken back into the local congregation to strengthen the vitality and fruitfulness of the local church so that our congregations can be more effective in making disciples of Jesus Christ. Also discuss ways that this knowledge may be used beyond the local congregation in the community.

While training takes the most effort in leading your lay servant ministries system, there are other components that need your attention as well.

Sending

Opportunities flow from ministry needs; and from ministry needs, we can interpret the equipping needs of the conference or district. Some questions to ask as we help lay servants find opportunities are:

- How do we love God, love others, serve the world, and help change lives in Jesus Christ?
- How do we make our congregations more vital and fruitful in making new disciples of Jesus Christ for the transformation of the world?
- What is it that we do as leaders within the church, caregivers in our congregations, or as communicators of the gospel that contributes to transformation?

Many lay servants feel they do not have enough opportunities to serve in their local congregations. Therefore, lay servants from one large church started a laity-led Wednesday night service that became an institution in their church. Others have held Lenten midweek worship services employing lay servants from across the district to supply the gifts and skills needed. Yet others have an annual lay-led tent revival and lead vacation Bible schools for churches too small to staff their own. Opportunities abound to match skills to service, but they take effort and planning.

Developing Service Opportunities

Many lay servants are passionate about ministries such as prison ministry, music, safe water, and food ministries, UMM, UMW, Nothing But Nets, connectional giving, mentoring, tutoring, Habitat for Humanity, and others. Some desire to organize and run retreats for organizations. Offer your lay servants the opportunity to become part of a speakers' bureau and then develop a brochure to advertise in churches, communities, and service clubs.

Creating a website and putting vignettes on YouTube.com is an excellent way to advertise speakers.

While the *Book of Discipline* encourages lay servants to take the initiative in finding ways to employ their skills for service, some do better than others, since some environments are more conducive than others to a person's set of skills. Conference and/or district directors can play a major role in directing and aiding lay servants in finding meaningful ministries to employ their services.

As conference and district directors, in cooperation with the conference and district lay leaders, you are in a prime position to see the needs of the district or annual conference. What volunteer positions are there that a certified lay servant, certified lay speaker, or certified lay minister may be gifted and equipped to fill? What have you heard from the district superintendents about the needs for mission and ministry that could be led by a lay servant with a passion in that area?

Service Ideas. There are a number of roles that lay servants can play in congregations, but these require initiative on their part. Consider downloading job descriptions from the Discipleship Ministries website and discussing them with lay servants at upcoming classes. Those discussions will generate many more ideas for service.

Annual Conference Suggestions. Create a missional attitude in the conference. If we are not teaching, encouraging, and nurturing in ways that lead our lay servants and churches to think outwardly and make new and transforming disciples of Jesus Christ, why are we talking about it?

District Suggestions. Small churches may not have all the skills to enhance their vitality. Survey your lay servants and advertise those who can be made available to other congregations in the areas of mentoring, leadership, worship, music, audiovisual assistance, and so on. Create working groups among the lay servants to exchange and enhance skills. Involve lay servants in pastor recognition and encouragement activities within the district.

Local Congregation Suggestions. Create a culture of accountability. Develop class meetings within local congregations. Lay servants can be trained to fulfill the role of class leader, and pastors can be given guidelines for supporting class leaders in their congregations. Lay servants can also start and lead Covenant Discipleship groups within their congregations. Lay servants can search for ways in which to strengthen the ministry of pastors to make them all God calls them to be. Many lay servants have gifts for worship and could involve themselves in worship committees, worship, or helping the pastor organize new and/or more Christ-encountering, life-changing worship experiences. Lay servants can teach a spiritual gifts course in their congregations. It is vital to find ways to identify, lift up, nurture, mentor, and train leaders and participants in all facets of lay ministry within your churches.

Community Outreach Suggestions. Find ways to contact local business owners, develop a relationship with them, and seek ways to work with, support, and encourage them. Talk to leaders in local schools to discover ways that lay servants can help organize efforts to provide for needs such as tutoring services, after-school programs, and backpack ministries. Meet with local government officials or social agencies to discuss needs such as working with families of prisoners, developing a plan to protect community gardens and green spaces, and finding ways to support the local police, fire departments, and the public library.

Skills Inventory. No person is better placed than the district director to know the skills available in the district laity; however, this takes effort and record keeping (see *Administration and Record Keeping*). Some conferences have modified their annual report forms to include primary and alternate preferred missions/ministries. A good way to capture this is to survey participants on the event evaluation about their areas of passion and their spiritual gifts. Over the course of two or three reporting periods, the district can amass a great list of lay servants and ministries that can be used across the district. While the emphasis is on local congregations, not all churches have the skills they need for ministry. The inventory helps find certified lay servants, certified lay speakers, and certified lay ministers who may be able and willing to serve beyond their local church to meet ministry needs of other churches.

Inclusiveness

Always be aware that diversity and inclusiveness enrich your programs. Make sure that everyone has the opportunity to be served by your lay servant programs. This may require efforts to teach courses in different languages. Lay servants of all backgrounds and cultural contexts need to be equipped to serve diverse communities.

Funding

It costs money to run the lay servant ministries program. Be prepared to build a budget with your lay servant ministries committee to submit to the person responsible for approving your budget. Become familiar with the district and conference budget cycles. An easy way to build a budget is to make the training events self-funded. The budget for the event includes funds for honoraria or expense reimbursement for facilitators, hospitality expenses (food, beverages, etc.), the cost of materials and resources, and building or janitorial expenses for the host site. Charge enough per participant to cover these costs. Both conferences and districts should consider small scholarships to help defray the costs for those who may not be able to afford the fees. Other costs for special events or other lay servant expenses outside the course events (such as expenses for committee meetings) go into the committee's district or conference budget. Some annual conferences manage finances at the district level, while others handle registration and expenses at the conference level, charging sufficient fees to self-fund the entire lay servant ministries program.

It is recommended that district directors strive to attend an ACDLSM Convocation at least once every three years. Travel expenses and fees for conference events and ACDLSM Convocations should also be budgeted (see Association of Conference Directors of Lay Servant Ministries on page 37).

Partnering

Lay servant ministries must be a ministry of collaboration at all levels. The United Methodist Church is a denomination that values the priesthood of all believers and the partnership between clergy and laity who are called to ministry. Without such partnership, the mission of The United Methodist Church falters. The directors of lay servant ministries need to foster these partnerships. Partnership occurs when clergy and laity teams facilitate, when pastors mentor lay servants, and when pastors meet with lay servants to jointly prepare their annual reports. Partnership also occurs when laity and clergy join in ministry at the local church level and beyond in leading, caring, or communicating.

District directors need to work in close harmony with the district superintendent and pastors in the district. Conference directors need to develop relationships with the district superintendents across the conference (annual conference is a great opportunity). Conference directors should ask the bishop for a time at the cabinet meeting to talk about the program. Make sure that both the bishop and conference staff know the purpose and direction of this important and vital leadership development program.

Best Practices

One of the best ways to satisfy *The Book of Discipline* requirement that district directors provide for ministry opportunities for lay servants is to organize regional or district associations or cluster groups. These groups or associations would meet monthly or quarterly, as needed, and follow a program of prayer, training, support, and encouragement. They would work within the context of the ministry settings that are in each district or conference addressing the opportunities and needs that arise and would be available for those who are lay servants.

All lay servants would be asked to attend these meetings and share their experiences, their gifts and graces, and their expectations with one another in a setting that is nonconfrontational and supportive. Each meeting consists of an opening devotion or extended prayer time, honoring the requests of those attending with their personal prayers, a time of sharing and expectation of ministry, and concludes with a training session that addresses one or more aspects of leading, caring, or communicating, or some of the ministry areas available in the district. Content of the training would change at each meeting as needed. Most important, the meetings can also address the spiritual development of those attending. If lay servants are not spiritual leaders, then something is definitely missing!

These cluster groups or associations serve as a way of ascertaining the spiritual gifts and abilities of the lay servants. They serve as a pool of teachers or trainers for district or conference events, and they may be the people who serve on the district or conference committee on lay servant ministries.

The district director can also monitor the development of each lay servant, guide and provide mentoring for those who need it, and give the director confidence in and knowledge of those who can be easily recommended for the role of lay speaker (pulpit supply).

Administrative Tasks and Recordkeeping

Any good leader knows that he or she must perform timely tasks to keep things in order. The following is a short list of important administrative tasks the conference or district director must accomplish. Delegation of duties not only helps with the workload but also creates a cooperative ministry environment.

- Manage meeting schedules for committees, associations, or cluster groups; be prepared to lead meetings with a spiritual tone, providing devotions and prayers.
- Record the minutes and other details of committee meetings.
- Establish and distribute a calendar of events and commitments, as needed.

- Maintain a list of courses used in prior years, instructors' information, and event details.
- Keep contact lists.
- Monitor Facebook, Twitter, and other social networking accounts.
- Establish and update a database of all lay servants—information, status, course, and compliance tracking.
- Save all annual reports for a minimum of five years.
- Act as a repository for the history of the conference or district.
- Plan any celebrations, such as dinners or luncheons, and order any awards of recognition.

Make use of formatted software programs such as databases, note pages, and task lists. Send meeting reminders by e-mail and text when possible. New ways of meeting online are also available (SKYPE, GoToMeeting, Google Hangouts, conference calls, etc.). Include any of these methods in your communication plans if time or distance is an issue. Be an innovative administrator.

There may be other tasks you must assume and complete, depending upon your specific ministry context. Enlist the aid of others, and let them share leadership responsibilities. Always work as a team, not as a lone wolf. The position of chairperson is not one of power, as much as it is one of servanthood. Remember, celebrations are as important as meetings, so champion and encourage lay servants.

Asset Based Community Development

Asset Based Community Development, also known as ABCD, is a method used to develop communities by determining what assets are available in the surrounding community. Assets include people, places, and organizations.

As you are planning for lay servant ministries activities, events, and service, look around you. What or who is available in your area? Do you need a location for an event? Look around the area for places that would provide a good venue. You may not find a United Methodist church, with the proper facility, but a church of another denomination might have what you need. Or you might find an organization nearby that has a good facility. Become partners with various congregations and organizations within the community. Invite the members of other congregations or employees of an organization to attend or participate in your courses.

There are many possibilities if you just look around and open your eyes and ears to them.

Continuous Improvement

Every process or event in the lay servant ministries system can be improved with an intentional and deliberate team that prays together and then discerns God's direction for mission or ministry. One way to vision the work of your committee is to use the Appreciative Inquiry Process—4 D Cycle:

- Discover: Appreciate what is going well—evaluate
- Dream: Imagine what might be.
- Design: Determine what should be.
- Deliver: Create what will be.

Then continue the cycle of discovering, dreaming, designing, and delivering. All this planning is based on an affirmative topic—what is going well in the process?

Each cycle works best on outcomes you can measure objectively, but the committee can also make judgments about how the lay servant ministries system might be improved. As you set goals for improvement, keep in mind the criteria to be met in order to meet your goals. In other words, be SMART and make your goals measurable!

Effective SMART goals are:

- **Specific:** Clear and unambiguous. They answer the five "W: questions—*What, Why, Who, Where,* and *Which*?
- **Measureable:** These goals answer the questions—How many, How much, and How will I know when it is accomplished?

- **Achievable:** Is the goal realistic? Can it be accomplished?
- **Relevant:** Is the goal worthwhile? Does it match our needs/efforts? It is not a good idea to measure something that is meaningless!
- **Timely:** What is the time frame for the goal to be met? What is the target date?

Action Steps

Action steps are the specific things you will do to accomplish your goals. Goal setting is helpful only if you discuss and plan the steps necessary to achieve those goals. Based on the goals that are set, your action steps are designed to get you where you have said you want to be.

If your goal is to become more inclusive, what will you need to do to make sure that it happens? The action steps may be to contact leaders in congregations where there is great diversity and ask them to suggest people who would provide diversity to your group. Invite those individuals to be on the lay servant ministries committee. Decide who will be responsible for contacting the congregational leader, whom you will invite, what you will say, how you will make people feel welcome.

Every element of the lay servant ministries system can be subject to continuous improvement, and every element needs to be subjected to the question, *"What can we do better to call, equip, and send our lay servants to better serve their congregations and communities?"* As you design your action steps, make sure you set a time to review how they are going. This becomes a system of planning, doing, checking, acting, and then planning again to seek new ways to better call, equip, and send the lay servants in your charge. The "Deming-Plan-Do-Check-Act" cycle is elegant in its simplicity and at its best when prayer precedes and supports the cycle (Henry R. Neave, *The Deming Dimension*, SBC Press, 1990):

- **Plan:** Design or revise the processes to improve results.
- **Do:** Implement the plan and measure the performance. How well did it work?

- **Check:** Assess the measurements and report results.
- **Act:** Decide on changes needed to improve the process.

Setting Your Committee Meetings

Prepare an e-mail distribution list for your district or conference committee members. Try giving a choice of several dates for the meeting. Be clear about the time and location. Arrange for childcare as needed. Make sure that the meeting site is handicap-accessible as needed for your committee members. Begin the meeting on time. Be respectful of the committee members' time.

Suggested Agenda for the Organizational Meeting

1. Opening devotions/singing. Set the stage for Christian conferencing.
2. Explain the purpose of the meeting.
3. Introduce the members of the committee.
4. Discuss the purpose and responsibilities of the committee and its role in lay servant ministries.
5. Explain the anticipated outcomes. Use these for the goals you wish to accomplish.
6. Compare the purpose of this committee with that of other district or conference committees (see Conference Committee on Lay Servant Ministries on page 24 or District Committee on Lay Servant Ministries on page 26).
7. Discuss the plan to reach your goals or expected outcomes. Use the Appreciative Inquiry Assessment sheets in the Appendix.
8. Plan for the second meeting. Schedule the meeting now, if possible. Define its purpose (initial identification of planning or training needs). Consider inviting a youth and/or young adult to participate in the planning. Finally, discuss the frequency of meetings.

9. End with singing and "A Covenant Prayer in the Wesleyan Tradition," *The United Methodist Hymnal*, 607.

During the meeting, take time out for prayer and discernment during difficult discussions or sticking points.

You may try the *CAP Experience* (Challenges, Assets and Abilities, Potential Partners) process during this initial meeting to help guide the discussion:

- **Challenges:** Current reality, changes needed.
- **Assets and Abilities:** Spiritual gifts, personal or material resources, opportunities, programs, etc.
- **Potential Partners:** Clergy, other organizations in the conference/district, communities who could partner to provide resources.

As part of the work of the lay servant ministries committee, you should always remember to:

- develop or review your mission and vision.
- review strategic initiatives of the annual conference.
- define measurable goals.
- develop plans of action.
- evaluate progress.

ASSOCIATION OF CONFERENCE DIRECTORS OF LAY SERVANT MINISTRIES (ACDLSM)

The Association of Conference Directors of Lay Servant Ministries exists to support and enable conference and district directors of lay servant ministries in their leadership roles. The association is an advocate and advisor for lay servant ministries, and it receives support from Discipleship Ministries (the General Board of Discipleship). It enables and promotes the partnership in ministry between the laity and clergy to fulfill the work of Jesus Christ. All current conference directors of lay servant ministries of The United Methodist Church may be members of this association. The immediate past president of the association, the liaison from Discipleship Ministries (General Board of Discipleship), and the president of the Association of Annual Conference Lay Leaders are also members of the ACDLSM and its executive committee. Immediate past conference and district directors are associate members who may attend meetings with voice but without vote. Current district directors are also invited to attend the annual meetings as nonvoting members.

The president, vice president, secretary, and treasurer are elected from the membership for two-year terms. They may succeed themselves for one additional term. The standing committees are the education committee, legislation committee, and the communications committee. Chairs are appointed from the membership by the president. Committee members may include associate members of the ACDLSM.

The executive committee is composed of the elected officers, the immediate past president, the committee chairs, the current president of the Association of Annual Conference Lay Leaders (AACLL), and the liaison from Discipleship Ministries. The executive committee has advisory powers as well as the power to act for the association between meetings.

Association dues are payable each year and should be covered by the annual conferences. Please check with the treasurer of the ACDLSM for the current amount due. Notify your annual conference treasurer of this required payment.

The Certified Lay Speaker

Directors of lay servant ministries need to offer equipping classes and encourage the development of preaching skills–as demonstrated through spiritual gifts–to meet the needs of the conference or district for lay servants called specifically to pulpit supply.

Suggestions for Conference and District Directors

Develop a lay speaker track that includes the appropriate courses as listed in *The Book of Discipline* (¶ 267)—leading worship, leading prayer, discovering spiritual gifts, preaching, United Methodist heritage, and United Methodist polity. The conference committee on lay servant ministries has the latitude to add other courses. Since most of the courses listed are of general interest to all lay servants, it would be beneficial to offer one or more of them in the spring and fall each year. Conference planning should ensure that they are taught more than once in any three-year cycle and that they are properly advertised throughout the conference so that lay servants have an opportunity to complete the educational requirements in a timely manner. In addition, all the courses with the exception of Introduction to Lay Ministry: The BASIC Course and the preaching courses are now offered online through BeADisciple.com as an alternative way to complete the required courses.

- Encourage pastors to mentor lay speakers and to give them opportunities to preach from their local pulpit while the pastor is there. If that opportunity seems limited, district directors might hold quarterly special preaching sessions where lay servants can come together to preach to and evaluate one another, refining their favorite sermons in readiness for supply opportunities in the upcoming quarter.
- Use video in all preaching classes to allow self-evaluation of sermons, but also to develop YouTube clips that can be used by pastors when seeking supply speakers and by the district committee on lay servant ministries for lay speaker certification interviews.
- To encourage upgrading skills, to foster accountability, and to assist in their examination of candidates, it is recommended that committees establish considerations or criteria that allow them to evaluate the effort, quality, and performance of the candidates. Such a system avoids arbitrary decisions and fosters objectivity and should include grace.
- Provide a list of recommended lay speakers for pulpit supply to the district office so that, in case of short notice, quality speakers can be designated. Certified lay servants who desire to fill pulpits or those pursuing certification as lay speakers would be eligible for the roster.
- Consider interviewing twice a year during advanced course training since many of the participants would be assembled. Although recommendation comes from the district committee

on lay servant ministries, certification comes from the conference committee on lay servant ministries. Certificates for successful completion of the lay speaker track or process are available at www.umcdiscipleship.org/laity. The presentation of a lay speaker pin is a way to recognize this accomplishment.

- Offer opportunities for continuing education. Continuous improvement of clergy and laity has long been a part of the Methodist tradition. Courses on pastoral and leadership development and other courses can help the committee understand the effort and commitment put forth by the candidates.

Suggested Interview Questions

By Church Council or Charge Conference. It is recommended that Wesley's historic questions be used by the church council or charge conference when considering someone who is seeking to be certified as a lay speaker. These questions do not need to be asked, but they should be part of the consideration process as the group reflects on the candidate:

1. *Do they know God as a pardoning God? Have they the love of God abiding in them? Do they desire nothing but God? Are they holy in all manner of conversation?*
2. *Have they gifts, as well as evidence of God's grace, for the work? Have they a clear, sound understanding; a right judgment in the things of God; a just conception of salvation by faith? Do they speak justly, readily, clearly?*
3. *Have they fruit? Have any been truly convinced of sin and converted to God, and are believers edified by their service?*

As long as these marks occur in them, we believe they are called of God to serve. These we receive as sufficient proof that they are moved by the Holy Spirit. (2016 BOD ¶ 310.1.d.).

By District Committee on Lay Servant Ministries. Once a person has received the recommendations from his/her pastor and charge conference, has completed the required course work, and is appearing before the district committee on lay servant ministries (or its equivalent) for interview, it is recommended that Wesley's historic questions be considered again as well as specific questions concerning the person's effectiveness in ministry. The following is a list of suggested questions and talking points to be used during the interview:

- Tell us about your faith journey and your understanding of the call of God upon your life.
- How would you describe your understanding of God, Christ, and the work of the Holy Spirit?
- How have you experienced the presence of God in your ministry?
- Tell us about a leadership experience you have had in the local church within the last year.
- Share with us a conflict in which you have been involved and how you dealt with it.
- Tell us how your service in your local church has demonstrated your appreciation of the history, doctrine, polity, worship, and liturgy of The United Methodist Church.
- What gifts, skills, and abilities do you bring to ministry as a lay speaker?
- Where do you feel your ministry needs to be strengthened?
- What are you doing for personal spiritual growth?
- What are you doing to take care of yourself physically?

Considerations and Criteria for Lay Speaker Certification

Conference Committee on Lay Servant Ministries. When a person has completed the course requirements, received all the necessary recommendations, and has interviewed with the district committee on lay servant ministries, then the recommendation of the district committee moves to the conference committee on lay servant ministries for final approval and certification.

Considerations and Criteria

- Courses taken in the lay speaker track
- Additional courses taken beyond those in lay speaker track
- Supply opportunities they have had
- Satisfactory supply evaluations by the congregation served
- Ministries in the local church and beyond
- Devotional life

(None of the considerations or criteria are mandatory except the completion of the required lay speaker courses and recommendations established by the *BOD* and/or the committee.)

Recertification. After a person is certified as a lay speaker, every three years he or she must receive the endorsement of the local church charge conference and appear before the district committee on lay servant ministries (or its equivalent) for an interview and recommendation for recertification. Because a certified lay speaker is also a certified lay servant, a lay speaker is also to complete one advanced course every three years and submit an annual report to his/her church council or charge conference and committee on lay servant ministries.

Compensation of Lay Speakers. The certified lay speaker is a layperson and as such is not eligible for support by equitable compensation funds, benefits, or pensions that are provided for clergy members. It is entirely appropriate that lay speakers be provided an honorarium for the services they render and/or for expenses incurred, such as mileage.

The Certified Lay Minister

The primary intent for the position of certified lay minister (CLM) at its inception was to serve as a congregational leader in smaller churches as part of a ministry team under the supervision of a clergyperson. Certified lay ministers may preach the word and guide the program ministry and mission of a congregation. Certified lay ministers may provide leadership in many other contexts and have responsibility for other expressions of mission and ministry, both within the congregation and in the community, district, or annual conference. Specializations for CLMs are now available in several areas of ministry, including parish nursing and church planting. The certified lay minister is not intended for occasional pulpit supply.

Suggestions for Conference and District Directors

- Develop certified lay minister (CLM) training that includes all the components of CLM Modules I-IV:
  - **Call and Covenant for Ministry:** Understanding of theology and call for ministry, exploring spiritual gifts, and developing a ministry covenant. This training includes Introduction to Lay Ministry: The BASIC Course and the advanced course "Discover Your Spiritual Gifts." (*Minimum Time: 30 hours*)
  - **The Practice of Ministry:** Four sections on leading worship, preaching/sharing faith, discipleship ministries, and caring for a congregation. (*Minimum Time: 8 hours per section or 32 hours*)
  - **Organization for Ministry:** Focus on the leader's task of organizing a congregation for mission and ministry. It provides specific guidance on topics central to a congregation's health. (*Minimum Time: 8 hours*)
  - **Connection for Ministry:** United Methodist theology, practice, and polity are explained with the roles of the local congregation, district, conference, and general church. (*Minimum Time: 8 hours*)

The conference committee on lay servant ministries has the latitude to add other courses or provide alternative training that is at least equivalent in time and contains all the components in the CLM Modules. Conference planning should ensure that training is regularly held, possibly once a year, and that the training is properly advertised throughout the conference so that certified lay servants will have an opportunity to complete the educational requirements in a timely manner. Each conference committee on lay servant ministries has the right to determine how the modules will be delivered and if it will allow a candidate to take the online modules offered by another annual conference.

- To encourage upgrading skills, to foster accountability, and to assist in the examination of candidates, establish considerations or criteria that allow the district committee on ordained ministry to evaluate the effort, quality, and performance of the candidate. Such a system avoids arbitrary decisions and fosters objectivity and should include grace.

- Provide an accurate roster of lay servants who have been certified as lay ministers to the board of ordained ministry for inclusion on the business of the annual conference report.

- Encourage the district committee on ordained ministry to interview in a timely manner. Although the district committee on ordained ministry interviews and recommends the candidate, the certification comes from the conference committee on lay servant ministries. Certificates for successful completion of the certified lay minister process are available at www/umcdiscipleship.org/laity.

- Offer opportunities for continuing education. Continuous improvement of both clergy and laity has long been a part of the Methodist tradition and is invaluable for the growth and spiritual formation of the certified lay minister.

- Keep up-to-date on specializations for the certified lay minister. The specializations will be a further point of conversation in the evaluative process.

Suggested Interview Questions

By Church Council or Charge Conference. It is recommended that Wesley's historic questions be used by the church council or charge conference when considering someone for certified lay ministry. These questions do not need to be asked, but they should be part of the consideration process as the group reflects on the candidate:

1. *Do they know God as a pardoning God? Have they the love of God abiding in them? Do they desire nothing but God? Are they holy in all manner of conversation?*

2. *Have they gifts, as well as evidence of God's grace, for the work? Have they a clear, sound understanding; a right judgment in the things of God; a just*

conception of salvation by faith? Do they speak justly, readily, clearly?

3. *Have they fruit? Have any been truly convinced of sin and converted to God, and are believers edified by their service?*

As long as these marks occur in them, we believe they are called of God to serve. These we receive as sufficient proof that they are moved by the Holy Spirit. (2016 BOD ¶ 310.1.d.)

By District Committee on Ordained Ministry. Once a person has received the recommendations from his/her pastor and church council or charge conference and his/her district superintendent, has completed the required course work, and is appearing before the district committee on ordained ministry for interview and recommendation of certification or recertification as a CLM, it is recommended that Wesley's historic questions be asked again as well as specific questions concerning the person's effectiveness in ministry. The following is a list of suggested questions and talking points to be used by district committees on ordained ministry:

- Tell us about your faith journey and your understanding of the call of God upon your life.
- How would you describe your understanding of God, Christ, and the work of the Holy Spirit?
- How have you experienced the presence of God in your ministry?
- Tell us about a leadership experience you have had in the local church within the last year.
- Share with us a conflict in which you have been involved and how you dealt with it.
- Tell us how your service in your local church has demonstrated your appreciation of the history, doctrine, polity, worship, and liturgy of The United Methodist Church.
- What gifts, skills, and abilities do you bring to certified lay ministry?
- Describe the covenant you have developed with your mutual ministry team.
- Where do you feel your ministry needs to be strengthened?

- What are you doing for personal spiritual growth?
- What are you doing to take care of yourself physically?

Considerations and Criteria for Lay Minister Certification

Conference Committee on Lay Servant Ministries. When a person has completed the course requirements, received all the necessary recommendations, and has interviewed with the district committee on ordained ministry, the recommendation of the district committee moves to the conference committee on lay servant ministries for final approval and certification.

Recertification. After a person is certified as a lay minister, every two years he/she must complete a ministry review and receive the endorsement of the local PPRC, church council, or charge conference, obtain a recommendation from the district superintendent, complete continuing education requirements, and appear before the district committee on ordained ministry for an interview and recommendation for recertification. Because a certified lay minister is also a certified lay servant, a lay minister is also to complete one advanced course every three years and submit an annual report to his/her church council or charge conference and committee on lay servant ministries.

Considerations and Criteria

- Courses taken in the certified lay minister or speaker track
- Additional courses taken beyond those in the lay minister track
- Ministry opportunities they have had
- Satisfactory ministry evaluations by the congregation served
- Outreach ministries in the local church and beyond
- Devotional life

(None of the considerations or criteria are mandatory except the completion of the required certified lay minister courses and recommendations established by the *BOD* and/or the committee.)

Compensation of Lay Ministers. The certified lay minister is a layperson and as such is not eligible for support by equitable compensation funds, benefits, or pensions that are provided for clergy members. If a certified lay minister is a lay staff member of a church, circuit, or cooperative parish, the local congregation is encouraged to provide compensation. It is important to remember that taxes should be withheld appropriate to a layperson.

Training the Trainers Guide

Introduction

Dr. Glenna Kyker Brayton

One of the purposes of training as a trainer for courses related to lay servant ministries is to acquire the knowledge and skills needed for leading, caring, or communicating the Christian faith. You will want to discover, define, and deliver what pastors and others need and want in ministry. You can do this by providing quality training at the basic and advanced course levels for lay servants.

With this objective in mind, the material in this *Training the Trainers Guide* will assist the conference or district committee in developing quality, effective training events for instructor candidates. Remember that your class will engage the participants longer than the average Sunday school time or the length of a typical Bible study. It will be more involved than a sermon. Whether the class time is meaningful and valuable to the participants will largely depend on how well you have prepared. You will find that it is difficult, if not impossible, to keep a group interested in what you have to say if you have not planned carefully and do not help them to see how what you and they are doing together will benefit them.

Knowing that people learn in a variety of ways and the ability to recognize the preferred ways of learning among the participants in your group can help you plan for a more meaningful experience as you train others to lead groups.

Candidates for training as instructors should be Christ-centered and content-filled. Each should have completed or read Introduction to Lay Ministry: The BASIC Course and have an understanding of the Wesleyan quadrilateral, the common core of Christian beliefs, and United Methodist beliefs as stated in *The Book of Discipline*.

Everything trainers do and say becomes a model for instructors who will leave this session to go out and lead sessions of their own. What happens in your group will determine the quality of the advanced courses and BASIC course sessions offered in your district or conference. Take time to think through the suggestions made here. Reconfigure whatever material in this section you will use to make it fit your own leadership style.

Begin every step of preparation and presentation with prayer. Pray for guidance to respond to those things God has called you to do (Ephesians 2:10). Pray for each member of your group to be inspired anew to service, and ask God to give you contagious enthusiasm for serving God's purposes.

Remember to leave time at the end of the course for sharing information, completing the evaluation form, a footwashing or handwashing service (or some other type of commitment service), and closing prayer. A service of Holy Communion and the awarding of certificates of completion are often done jointly with participants and leaders of other courses in a closing worship service.

Training the Trainers Event

Dr. Diana L. Hynson, retired staff member of Discipleship Ministries

For District or Conference Planners

Lay servants offer a tremendous gift of ministry to the community of faith. The scope of lay-led ministry extends to every possible ministry area of the church. Many of those areas have specific lay servant/leader development courses to help prepare people for the ministries of teaching, evangelism, stewardship, visitation, or a host of other possibilities. We do not become proficient in these ministries by accident, nor by receiving a textbook-worth of information. We are taught, and we practice. Faithful and effective ministry requires faithful and effective leaders and teachers.

The purpose of this segment of the guide is to provide background information and a workshop plan for preparing leaders/facilitators of lay servant "Learning & Leading" courses.

Who Should Teach? Good teaching is part art and part practice; and it is a spiritual gift. A person with a great compendium of knowledge about a particular subject may not be the best teacher of that subject, although knowledge is important. Good teaching is about so much more than the transmission of content. An excellent teacher has a gift for drawing students in to the well of growth and learning and for drawing out the great depth of experience of the students for the benefit of all. Teaching is a deep emotional experience based on the trust of teacher and student alike. Learning occurs best in safe places. Look for these traits in teachers:

- a love of people
- a love of teaching
- patience and the ability to listen
- skill in giving instructions and explanations
- ability to maintain order in a group
- a commitment to purposeful creativity
- a commitment to continuous learning

Follow your district or conference guidelines, which may include, but are not limited to, requirements for

- gender, ethnic, and age balance among teaching candidates,
- balance of lay and clergy instructors (all of whom must attend training),
- previous participation in lay servant courses and/ or certification,
- membership in The United Methodist Church,
- familiarity with Wesleyan theology and history.

In an era of e-mail and instant messaging, you will need to decide the best way to invite trainer candidates. One thing has not changed, though, and that is the benefit of the personal touch. When a candidate has agreed to be a part of the teaching team, be sure to follow up that acceptance with a written note of thanks, including the details for the training and any advance preparation required.

Preparing for the Training Event. Ideally, you have a team that will help to recruit trainers and set up the training event. The planning team will:

- set the date, clearing it on the conference or district calendar as necessary.
- identify a location with easy access, sufficient parking, and good teaching facilities.
- identify and invite candidates to be trained.
- handle the logistics of budgeting, tuition, receipt of registrations, accounting, and class list.
- attend to hospitality needs.
- promote and advertise the event as needed.
- prepare training materials.
- recruit the workshop leader and handle travel, accommodations, and honorarium, as needed.
- prepare how to acknowledge or accredit completion of the training.

Facility Needs. Identify a facility with these criteria in mind:

- accessibility, both in terms of getting to the site and then within the site (non-negotiable).
- adequate lighting inside and out.
- comfortable table and chair arrangement.
- comfortable heating and cooling.
- adequate sound system for the size of the room.

- sufficiently removed from other activities so that participants can hear and concentrate.
- necessary AV or other technical equipment (and someone who knows how to use it).
- whiteboard or newsprint and markers available.
- unobstructed view of the instructor.
- sufficient room both for table set up and for easy movement for active teaching experiences.
- convenient place for meals and snacks.
- sufficient number of restrooms, including handicap-accessible facilities.

The best instructor and teaching plan in the universe cannot completely make up for a teaching space that is inhospitable and inadequate for learning.

HOSPITALITY NEEDS

- Have a hospitality team greet people as they arrive.
- Have light refreshments and/or coffee, tea, juice, and water at a convenient table.
- Provide a name tag for each person.
- Collect unpaid registration money or information.
- If you have prepared a packet with handouts and an agenda for the day, distribute them before the event begins.
- Be sure directions are clear for where to find the meeting space, restrooms, and any other area participants will need to go.
- If participants will need directions from the parking area to the correct entrance and meeting space, station greeters or post signs with that information.

The Teaching Plan

A Word to the Workshop Leader. We learn to teach by teaching, so an important part of this experience will be offering a creative teaching plan that imparts the information participants need and that can be analyzed as a model for how the teaching took place. In addition,

have participants bring a copy of a lay servant course they would like to teach.

This plan will make full use of a variety of intelligences and learning hooks that promote learning among a diverse group of learners. We tend to teach using the activities that support our preferred way of learning, but you are encouraged to teach the activities as they are written, especially if they stretch you to try new things. You may adapt the teaching plan as you need to, but be sure to substitute like activities. For example, if a particular activity using music won't work for you, substitute a different musical activity. If you are not a musical learner and feel you cannot effectively lead such an activity, having a teaching partner with complementary skills would be most helpful.

The instructions in the teaching plan are direct. They indicate what you should do or say without specifically supplying a script. If you find you need further resources, the lay servant course, *Teach Adults,* is similar in its aims to this workshop and may be used if you want more time and practical application.

Learning That Works. We remember what we have an emotional attachment to. Powerful memories evoke powerful emotions. In fact, the mysterious brain allows us to make rational decisions only when the emotive part of our brain is engaged.

We use existing information and experiences as building blocks for incoming information. We retain only what can hook into something that is already there; otherwise, we have no way to make any sense or meaning from new experiences. The more powerful the hook, the more memorable is the experience. This model will use a number of learning hooks and will deliberately identify them to help you in the session analysis.

Our brains need some variety, as well as periods of activity and rest. Change pace periodically from work that is intense to activities that are more relaxed. If everyone has been sitting, do something to make them move. When you return from a break, take two or three minutes to do some sort of "brain twister" that helps everyone refocus their attention. If you have a teaching partner or engage the learners in the teaching plan, the shift in leader is an obvious change of pace. This model will demonstrate ways to keep a sustainable rhythm.

Adults and teens will value the learning experience most when they have a stake in the process and its outcome. Children may need to have educational decisions made for them, but teens and adults prefer to have a say in that which concerns them. One way to keep interest and involvement high is to have participants set their own specific and measurable learning goals or develop a learning contract. Learning goals (in or beyond the class) might be:

- I will learn and gain comfort with teaching through two intelligences that are currently unfamiliar.
- I will learn to analyze teaching plans to make best use of a variety of learning hooks.

The learning goals of this teaching experience are listed at the beginning of the workshop plan. Participants may want instead to prepare their own learning contract or identify the degree to which they will pursue excellence in the learning goals already stated. A learning contract might include a commitment to engage in all discussion, including issues that are not well understood or to practice each new learning technique in or outside the class, as time and occasion permit.

Teen and Adult Learners. Teens, especially older ones, will have the same essential learning abilities as adults. They can think abstractly, reason deductively and inductively, set aside personal desires for the sake of the group, manage their own behavior, and so on. If you have teens in your group, the main accommodation you will make is in regard to their level of experience in life and in the church. Teenagers who are mature enough to teach a lay servant course are probably comfortable being front and center, yet they may lack the experience in group dynamics to do the essential crowd control or to handle difficult people adroitly (some adults don't do that very well, either). Regardless of the age or station of the participants, the class setting must be a safe place for everyone to risk trying new things, listening to honest feedback, and offering constructive criticism.

Watch also for the amount of church lingo and acronyms you or others use. Good teacher candidates who are not "cradle Methodists" may be less familiar with the acronyms and verbal shortcuts that longtimers take for granted.

Spiritual Leadership. No matter what you know or do, the group members will look at you as a spiritual leader. You are the teacher, and thus, the resident expert, but it is more important to be open to mutual learning. Everyone present brings something worthwhile to the teaching endeavor.

Your role is to be honest, authentic, and faithful. Freely admit what you do not know and commit to finding an answer. Part of the learning experience is analyzing and evaluating this teaching plan and your performance as a teacher. Welcome input from the other faithful participants and understand that you can learn from what goes well and also from what does not. In so doing, you model humility and grace.

Training the Trainers
One-Day Event
8:00 am—4:00 pm

Preparation

- ☑ Items for the focal point (see below).
- ☑ Name tags
- ☑ Print the "Get-Acquainted" activity and have multiple copies on each table (found in the Appendix of this resource and available for download at www.umcdiscipleship.org/laity under Lay Servant Ministries Resources).
- ☑ Handouts (downloaded and copied)
- ☑ Create posters of the eight core intelligences (see page 57) and display them around the room.
- ☑ Bible (multiple copies)
- ☑ Prepare for morning prayer
- ☑ Hymnals for each person
- ☑ Multiple copies of lay servant courses (plus the course guides others have brought)
- ☑ Search "multiple intelligences" on the Internet to find an inventory to use with the group, ahead of time, if possible (optional).
- ☑ Create a poster of learning hooks (see page 59 of this guide).
- ☑ Newsprint or whiteboard and markers
- ☑ Recruit four or five volunteers for a fishbowl exercise and prepare them for their roles ahead of time.

Workshop Goals

Participants will:

1. understand basic information about how people learn.
2. learn several learning hooks and how to employ them in a learning experience.
3. be able to analyze teaching activities to understand how and why they work.
4. learn basic information about classroom dynamics.
5. gain some skill and practice in leading a course.

Room Set Up

Use a room that has enough space for table groups and movement for standing group activities.

- Arrange tables and chairs for no more than eight people at a table. Be sure everyone can see the presenter. Participants need enough room to be comfortable for learning, and they should also be able to hear one another in small-group activities.
- Use one table for the leader's materials and as a focal point with items that support the ambiance of the learning setting—a small cross, an open Bible, or other visual aid. The presenter may also want a podium.
- Put up a poster for each of the learning styles to be used in the activity on learning styles.
- Arrange for a sound system if the size of the room and group require it.

8:00—8:30   Welcome, Gathering, Registration
- ☑ Encourage participants to get some refreshments and to find a seat.

☑ When three or four people have assembled at a table, ask them to work on the "Get Acquainted" activity until morning prayer.

8:30—9:00   Morning Prayer

The liturgy for morning prayer is 876 in *The United Methodist Hymnal*. A similar liturgy can be found on pages 8–9 in *The Upper Room Worshipbook*. Have a copy of the hymnal placed on the table for each person. The hymnals will be used during the workshop.

9:00—9:45   Understanding How People Learn

☑ Take a quick poll using these questions: Raise your hand if you . . .

1. often draw or doodle while listening in a meeting.
2. remember the story better from seeing the movie rather than reading the book.
3. remember the story better from reading the book rather than seeing the movie.
4. listen better with your eyes closed than by reading along.
5. recall information better when you have made a rhyme to go with it.
6. remember faces better than you recall names.
7. know better what you think when you work it out verbally with others.
8. figure out things better when left alone and no one is talking to you.
9. remember dates well but are hazy on the historical details.
10. need to see the map to get directions because just hearing directions won't do.
11. would rather just take the appliance apart to fix it than to read the owner's manual (and maybe have pieces left over).
12. remember the jingle better than you recall the product it goes with.

☑ Refer to the intelligence inventory, if you were able to use it, and also to the handout *Overview of the Eight Core Intelligences*. Agreements with the above statements suggest your learning preferences. Give the group about five minutes to look over the list to see what "sounds like them." Tell participants to put a checkmark by the intelligences that most identify them.

☑ Now ask people to stand by the poster of the intelligence that is their most preferred. Tell them that if there is a tie, they should choose one. After a moment, ask participants to move to the least preferred intelligence. Then have participants move to the intelligence that they can do, but do not particularly like.

Most likely, there was no universal agreement about the most or least preferred intelligences. The point is that they are different because people have different learning strengths and tend to follow those strengths when they teach. None of these are right or wrong; they just are.

☑ Have participants return to their tables. First, be sure that the activities associated with the various intelligences are understood, then discuss these questions:

1. As a student, what activities help you the most? the least?
2. As a teacher, what sort of teaching methods do you most employ? Are they consistent with your learning preferences?
3. If you teach using only your one or two learning preferences, what are the implications for the learners in the group who do not share those preferences?
4. What learning do you want to retain from this awareness of multiple intelligences and learning preferences?

9:45—10:30   Learning Hooks

☑ Post the "Learning Hooks" poster and distribute the "Learning Hooks" handout.
☑ Review the information and be sure everyone understands what each hook means.
☑ Assign the Scripture passages to the different table groups, one passage to a group. Group members should read their passage and identify seven learning hooks (one of each) that would work for the selected passage. Have groups work silently for the

first several minutes, then allow them to talk over the assignment within their table group. They can use the handout for recording the different learning hooks. Remind them that music can be used as a learning hook.

☑ When groups have their lists complete, start with one table and ask the participants to introduce their passage by way of the first learning hook (Find Common Ground). The next table will introduce their passage with the second hook (Use Questions). Continue through the list of learning hooks until you have at least one example of each hook and every table has reported at least once.

☑ As time allows, get more examples, then discuss any observations or questions. If it would be helpful, record the examples on newsprint for the review later.

10:30—10:45 BREAK

10:45—11:45 Classroom Dynamics

You will not address that subject fully, no matter what you do here. This segment, at best, can only introduce some common issues—regulating the flow of conversation to be sure everyone has a chance, dealing with monopolizers, drawing out the shy ones, being sensitive

to the teachable moments, placing learning above the lesson.

You will need four or five volunteers for this fishbowl exercise below. Ideally, the volunteers will become familiar with their roles ahead of time. The "teacher" in the fishbowl activity can either be you or one of the volunteers.

☑ Ask for group members to call out group dynamics issues, popcorn style, and record them on newsprint or whiteboard. (You will have to point out that time will not allow you to address all of them.)

☑ Take a few minutes to see what tips the group members can offer to one another.

☑ Call together your fishbowl volunteers. The rest of the group will observe, using the *Group Dynamics Worksheet* for notes. The fishbowl will dramatize a class session.

☑ The "teacher" will begin the "class" with the other volunteers as class members in keeping with the role they are assigned. Since this is something that you will not have prepared ahead of time, use a Scripture passage or issue with which you are familiar. Conduct the simulated class for fifteen to twenty minutes so that the observers get a good picture of the overall flow of the discussion and dynamics. Then open the fishbowl for the comments of the observers. Use the questions on the worksheet to start the discussion.

After the review of the observers, ask participants to comment on how they experienced the group dynamics.

Summarize the observations and point out where and how group leadership took place. Remember that

> **Intelligences used:** *Social (fishbowl group and review of the experience); Independent (observers took notes); Body/Kinesthetic (people acted out roles); Verbal (the conversation was the subject of the lesson)*
>
> **Learning Hooks:** *Create interest (a simulation rather than just a discussion); Find common ground (the simulated activity will probably feel very familiar); Connect learning to life (observers and fish bowl participants will probably see themselves in the activity and will gain insight into how to address a similar situation and may gain insight into their own patterns of behavior).*

this is a safe place, so talking about what did not go well can also be fruitful learning, too.

11:45—1:00   LUNCH AND BREAK (*adjust this time as necessary for the size of the group*)

1:00—2:45   Practice Teaching
This activity will use a Reflection/Action/Reflection pattern, starting with the lay servant course guides the participants brought with them or the extra copies you have on hand. If there are not enough copies to go around, the course guides can be shared in small groups. Remind everyone of the hymnals available.

☑ Ask group members to turn to session one within the lay servant course guides. (Distribute as needed.) Starting with the first session, identify the intelligences and learning hooks that are employed in the lesson plans. Visualize what each activity might look like in actual practice and take notes on how it engages the learner. Allow about twenty minutes for the review of the various course guides. Use the *Course Analysis Worksheet.*

☑ After the review, you can take several minutes for observations or just go directly into the practice teaching.

☑ Participants must choose an activity that is new for them. They may need to adapt or create a new activity to teach a particular lesson from the course guide. If possible, have no more than four or five persons to a group to maximize the opportunity for all to practice leading.

☑ Allow time for group members to prepare some segment to teach. Groups may want to take a five-minute break or stretch between preparation time and teaching time. For a group of five people, begin the practice teaching by at least 1:45 p.m. That will allow everyone at least ten minutes to guide one

> **Intelligences used:** *Social and Independent (review and preparation time; teaching time); Verbal (reading and reviewing the course guide); Visual and Verbal (use of the worksheet and course guides)*
>
> **Learning Hooks:** *observe and record*

teaching activity. Groups will review after the 2:45 p.m. break.

2:45—3:00   BREAK

3:00—4:00   Analysis and Review
☑ Ask individuals to work silently for five minutes to jot down notes about what they think worked and didn't work (and why) in their own presentations.

☑ Ask for responses as you did in the "Learning Hook" exercise. Go around the tables and ask for one response from each table; then repeat the rounds. Encourage clarity and brevity.

☑ Review the day's activities, starting with morning prayer. Recall the intelligences and the learning hooks that were used.

☑ If you need discussion starters, use these questions:

1. How well were the various intelligences and learning preferences represented during the day?
2. How often did you change the pace? What effect did that have on the learning experience?
3. What learning hooks were employed? Was there a variety? How did this affect the learning experience?
4. How did it feel to do something you had not tried before? How has your experience here helped you to teach creatively and effectively?

4:00   Closing

☑ Thank everyone for their participation.

☑ Make any necessary announcements.

☑ Close with a benediction.

Worksheets for the Training the Trainers course are available in the Appendix and may be downloaded from www.umcdiscipleship.org/laity under Lay Servant Ministries Resources (Group Dynamics Worksheet, Group Dynamics Roles Worksheet, and Course Analysis Worksheet—Training the Trainer).

Overview of the Eight Core Intelligences

Word Smart—Verbal/Linguistic

 Learners who are "word smart" enjoy working and playing with words and need verbal stimulation.

Some Verbal Learning Activities: reading • writing • telling stories • readers' theater • completing sentences • memorizing names/dates • writing poems • keeping a journal • debate • jokes

Number Smart—Logical/Mathematical

 Learners who are "number smart" enjoy numbers, patterns, and problem solving.

Some Logical/Mathematical Activities: number and word puzzles • exploring patterns, sequences, and relationships • step-by-step instructions • games • deciphering codes • outlining • learning what lies beneath the surface

Picture Smart—Visual/Spatial

 Learners who are "picture smart" enjoy seeing and visualizing things.

Some Visual/Spatial Activities: using pictures • imagining (see with our inner eye) • maps • graphs • charts • video or movies • understanding the relationships among things • drawing

Music Smart—Musical/Rhythmic

 "Music smart" learners receive information through music and rhythm (but do not necessarily have skill as a musician).

Some Musical/Rhythmic Activities: writing musical formulas for information • tapping out rhythms • listening to music while working • creating rap singing • playing instruments • using story songs • making a musical instrument

Body Smart—Body/Kinesthetic

 Learners who are "body smart" need to use movement and touch.

Some Body/Kinesthetic Activities: games requiring movement • dancing • marching • touching objects • pantomime • role playing/drama • using motions with songs or stories • sports

People Smart—Interpersonal or Social

 Social learners learn from and with others in small groups or teams

Some Social Learning Activities: interviews • discussion and dialogue • asking and answering questions • cooperative learning games • brainstorming • parties • service projects

Self-Smart—Intrapersonal or Independent

These learners work best on their own.

Some Independent Learning Activities: using reflection and self-knowledge • figuring out things for themselves • work in silence (for a while at least) • identifying with a character in a story • research project • focusing on inner feelings

Nature Smart—Naturalist

Naturalist learners appreciate nature/natural world, including the "heavens."

Some Naturalist Learning Activities: observing and interacting with nature/natural elements (living/not living) • categorizing order of things (species, types) • understanding relationship between patterns of growth/development and natural consequences • nature walk • work with pets or animals • learn outside • look at stars

Learning Hooks

Find Common Ground

Identify an area of mutual experience.

Use Questions

Questions help make connections with new and current information. Use a variety of questions—for information, analysis, synthesis, clarification, and so on.

Draw on Prior Knowledge

This entails including what we may not realize we know. You can start with, "Tell me all you know about . . ."

Expose Misconceptions

Everyone gets some things confused or misunderstands. Information changes, and we don't always keep up-to-date. This is OK; we just need to clarify.

Clarify Vocabulary

Your vocabulary, biblical text, student book material, reference material, information from the Internet, church and theological terms, other specialized terms—be sure everyone is on the same page.

Create Interest

Be creative. Approach an old subject in a new way. Take an opposite approach. Come in through the "back door." Play the devil's advocate. Bring up a little known fact. Find a weird or ironic point.

Connect Learning to Life

Linking lessons to real life is what makes them stick. Conversely, irrelevant information and activities don't stick. This is the "so what" that makes the lesson worthwhile.

- Genesis 11:1-9 (The Tower of Babel)
- 1 Kings 3:16-28 (The wisdom of Solomon)
- Jeremiah 29:1-9 (From Jeremiah's letter to the Exiles)
- Matthew 5:43-48 (Love your enemy)
- John 15:1-11 (Jesus, the true vine)
- Philippians 4:10-14 (Being content in the circumstance)

Suggested Resources

The Book of Discipline of The United Methodist Church, United Methodist Publishing House (Current Edition)

Spiritual Formation

- *Spiritual Preparation for Christian Leadership*, E. Glenn Hinson, Upper Room Books, 1999
- *John Wesley: Holiness of Heart and Life*, Charles Yrigoyen Jr., Abingdon Press, 1999
- *Becoming Barnabas, the Ministry of Encouragement*, Paul Moots, Rowman & Littlefield, 2004
- *The Soul of Tomorrow's Church*, Kent Ira Groff, Upper Room Books, 2000

Leading Meetings

- *Discerning God's Will Together: A Spiritual Practice for the Church*, Danny E. Morris & Charles M. Olsen, Rowman & Littlefield, Revised and Updated Edition, 2012
- *Hearing with the Heart*, Debra K. Farrington, Josey-Bass, 2002

Appreciative Inquiry

- *The Thin Book of Appreciative Inquiry*, Sue Annis Hammond, Thin Book 3rd edition, 2013
- *Appreciative Inquiry Handbook: For Leaders of Change*, David L. Cooperrider, Diana Whitney, and Jacqueline Stavros, Berrett-Koehler Publishers, Inc., 2008
- *Memories, Hopes, and Conversations: Appreciative Inquiry and Congregational Change*, Mark Lau Branson, Alban Institute, 2004

Asset-Based Community Development

- *Building Communities from the Inside Out: A Path Toward Finding and Mobilizing a Community's Assets*, John L. McKnight and John P. Kretzmann, ACTA Publishing, 1993
- *The Power of Asset Mapping: How Your Congregation Can Act on Its Gifts*, Luther Snow, Rowman & Littlefield, 2004
- *ABCD in Action: When People Care Enough to Act (pdf)*, Mike Green, ABCD Trainer, http://www.mike-green.org/pub/abcd_book_introduction.pdf

Mission and Ministry

- *Introducing the Missional Church: What It Is, Why It Matters, How to Become One*, Alan J. Roxburgh and M. Scott Boren, Baker Books, 2009
- *Missional Renaissance: Changing the Scorecard for the Church*, Reggie McNeal, Josey-Bass, 2009
- *The Forgotten Ways*, Alan Hirsch, Brazos Press, 2nd edition, 2016

- *Missional: Joining God in the Neighborhood,* Alan J. Roxburgh, Baker Books, 2011
- *Touch: Pressing Against the Wounds of a Broken World*, Rudy Rasmus, Thomas Nelson Publishing, 2008
- *Not Just a One-Night Stand: Ministry with the Homeless*, John Flowers, Karen Vannoy, Upper Room Books, 2009
- *Five Practices of Fruitful Congregations,* Robert Schnase, Abingdon Press, 2007

Certificates and Forms

Lay Servant Ministries certificates and forms are available for download at www.umcdiscipleship.org/laity (see Appendix)

Appendix

CERTIFIED LAY SERVANT ANNUAL REPORT

TO THE CHARGE CONFERENCE

Initial Application or Request for Renewal

Report for year ending _____

(Part 1) DATA ON THE LAY SERVANT

Name (Mrs. ___ Ms. ___ Mr. ___) _____

Address _____

City/State/Zip _____

Telephone (H) _____ (C) _____

E-mail _____

Name of District _____

Name of Church _____

Church Address _____

City/State/Zip _____

Church Telephone _____

(Part 2) STATUS OF THE LAY SERVANT

For initial application as a certified lay servant ( )

    1. What year did you complete your basic course? _____

    2. What year did you complete your advanced course? _____

    3. What was the title of your advanced course? _____

For renewal as a certified lay servant ( )

    1. What year did you complete your last advanced course? _____

    2. What was the title of your last advanced course? _____

(Part 3)   REQUEST OF THE LAY SERVANT

I request recommendation of my pastor and my church council/charge conference to begin/renew as a certified lay servant for the ensuing year.

Date _____ Lay Servant _____

(Part 4)   RECOMMENDATION OF THE PASTOR

I recommend concurrence with the request of this person to begin/renew as a certified lay servant for the ensuing year.

Date _____ Pastor _____

(Part 5)   RECOMMENDATION OF THE CHURCH COUNCIL/CHARGE CONFERENCE

The church council/charge conference of _____ (church/charge) recommends the above person begin/renew as a certified lay servant for the ensuing year.

Date _____ Church Council Chair or District Superintendent _____

(To be completed by those requesting renewal as certified lay servants)

(Part 6)   MINISTRIES BY THE LAY SERVANT

During the past year, I have participated in *caring ministries* as follows:

____ served as a volunteer in a caregiving institution

____ provided one-on-one caring

____ at a hospital, nursing home, or to a shut-in

____ in membership/evangelism visitation

____ served in caring/outreach projects (food pantry, prison ministry, etc.)

____ other caring activities (Please list) _____

During the past year, I have participated in *leading ministries* as follows:

____ served as member of committee, board, commission, council, task force, etc.

____ served as a volunteer at a community agency

____ at my local church

____ beyond my local church

____ on my District __ Conference __ Jurisdiction __ General Church level

____ other leading activities (Please list) _____

During the past year, I have participated in *communicating ministries* as follows:

____ served as worship leader in _____ services

_____ delivered _____ devotional messages

_____ taught _____ classes

_____ shared my faith story _____

_____ brought message in _____ worship services

_____ other speaking activities (Please list) _____

During the past year, I have participated in additional opportunities for ministry as follows:

_____

(Part 7)   PERSONAL AND SPIRITUAL GROWTH BY THE LAY SERVANT

In what activities have you engaged and/or what books have you read or used during the past year to help you develop your devotional life; improve your understanding of the Bible; improve your understanding of The United Methodist Church; and improve your skills in caring, leading, communicating, and speaking?

_____

(Part 8)   FEEDBACK BY THE LAY SERVANT

Do you feel called to be in service in any area of ministry, either in the church or outside the church, in which you are not currently involved? __ yes __ no If yes, please list those areas below: _____

_____

What additional training or support do you need or would you suggest to further your ministry: _____

_____

Give any recommendations you have for improving lay servant ministries in your district or conference: _____

_____

Note: District directors are encouraged to respond to any comments within this section.

CERTIFIED LAY SPEAKER ANNUAL REPORT

TO THE CHARGE CONFERENCE

Initial Application or Request for Renewal

Report for year ending _____

> **NOTICE:** After this form is completed and signed, the recording secretary of the church council or charge conference is requested to reproduce THREE copies: (1) lay servant, (2) district director of lay servant ministries, (3) district superintendent. The recording secretary of the church council or charge conference keeps the ORIGINAL. (Revised December 2016)

(Part 1) DATA ON THE LAY SPEAKER

Name (Mrs. __ Ms. __ Mr. __) _____

Address _____

City/State/Zip _____

Telephone (H) _____ (C) _____

E-mail _____

Name of District _____ Name of Church _____

Church Address _____

City/State/Zip _____ Church Telephone _____

(Part 2) STATUS OF THE LAY SPEAKER

For initial application as a certified lay speaker ( )

   1. Are you currently a certified lay servant? _____ yes _____ no

   2. What year did you complete your basic course? _____

   3. What year did you complete your advanced course for certification as a lay servant? _____

   4. What was the title of your advanced course? _____

   5. Which of the following required lay speaking courses have been completed?

         Leading Worship _____ Leading Prayer _____ Discovering Spiritual Gifts _____
         Preaching _____ United Methodist Heritage _____ United Methodist Polity _____

(Upon completion of the required course work, the lay speaker candidate will be examined by the district committee on lay servant ministries and recommended to the conference committee on lay servant ministries to be considered for certification.)

For renewal as a certified lay speaker ( )

    1. What year did you first become certified as a lay speaker? _____

    2. Date of last review of lay speaker status: _____ Approved: _____ yes _____ no

    3. What year did you complete your last advanced course? _____

    4. What was the title of your last advanced course? _____

(Part 3)   REQUEST OF THE LAY SPEAKER

I request recommendation of my pastor and my charge conference to begin/renew as a certified lay speaker for the ensuing year.

Date _____ Lay Servant _____

(Part 4)   RECOMMENDATION OF THE PASTOR

I recommend concurrence with the request of this person to begin/renew as a certified lay speaker for the ensuing year.

Date _____ Pastor _____

(Part 5)   RECOMMENDATION OF THE CHURCH COUNCIL/CHARGE CONFERENCE

The church council/charge conference of _____ (church/charge) recommends the above person begin/renew as a certified lay speaker for the ensuing year.

Date _____ Church Council Chair or District Superintendent _____

(To be completed by those requesting renewal as a lay speaker)

(Part 6)   MINISTRIES BY THE LAY SPEAKER

During the past year, I have participated in *caring ministries* as follows:

_____ served as a volunteer in a caregiving institution

_____ provided one-on-one caring

_____ at a hospital, nursing home, or to a shut-in

_____ in membership/evangelism visitation

_____ served in caring/outreach projects (food pantry, prison ministry, etc.)

_____ other caring activities (Please list) _____

During the past year, I have participated in *leading ministries* as follows:

_____ served as member of committee, board, commission, council, task force, etc.

_____ served as a volunteer at a community agency

_____ served at my local church

_____ served beyond my local church

_____ served on my district __ conference __ jurisdiction __ general church level

_____ other leading activities (Please list) _____

During the past year, I have participated in *communicating ministries* as follows:

_____ brought message in _____ worship services

_____ served as worship leader in _____ services

_____ delivered _____ devotional messages

_____ taught _____ classes

_____ shared my faith story _____

_____ other speaking activities (Please list) _____

During the past year, I have participated in additional opportunities for ministry as follows:

_____

(Part 7)   PERSONAL AND SPIRITUAL GROWTH BY THE LAY SPEAKER

In what activities have you engaged and/or what books have you read or used during the past year to help you develop your devotional life; improve your understanding of the Bible; improve your understanding of The United Methodist Church; and improve your skills in caring, leading, communicating, and speaking?

_____

(Part 8)   FEEDBACK BY THE LAY SPEAKER

Do you feel called to be in service in any area of ministry, either in the church or outside the church, in which you are not currently involved? _____ yes _____ no. If yes, please list those areas below: _____

_____

What additional training or support do you need or would suggest to further your ministry: _____

_____

Give any recommendations you have for improving lay servant ministries in your district or conference: _____

_____

CERTIFIED LAY MINISTER ANNUAL REPORT

TO THE CHARGE CONFERENCE

Initial Application or Request for Renewal

Report for year ending _____

> **NOTICE:** After this form is completed and signed, the recording secretary of the charge conference is requested to reproduce THREE copies: (1) lay speaker, (2) district director of lay servant ministries, (3) district superintendent. The recording secretary of the charge conference keeps the ORIGINAL.
> **(Revised December 2016)**

(Part 1)   DATA ON THE CERTIFIED LAY MINISTER

Name (Mrs. __ Ms. __ Mr. __) _____

Address _____

City/State/Zip _____

Telephone (H) _____ (C) _____

E-mail _____

Name of District _____ Name of Church _____

Church Address _____

City/State/Zip _____ Church Telephone _____

(Part 2)   STATUS OF THE CERTIFIED LAY MINISTER

For initial application as a certified lay minister ( )

1. Are you currently a certified lay servant? _____ yes _____ no

2. What year did you complete your basic course? _____

3. What year did you complete your advanced course for certification as a lay servant? _____

4. What was the title of your advanced course? _____

5. Which of the following required modules have been completed?

   Module 1: Call and Covenant for Ministry _____ Module 2: The Practice of Ministry _____

   Module 3: Organization for Ministry _____   Module 4: Connection for Ministry _____

(Upon completion of the required course work and after completion of appropriate screening and assessment, the CLM candidate requests a letter of recommendation from his/her district superintendent. The CLM candidate then applies in writing and appears before the district committee on ordained ministry for interview and recommendation for certification.)

For recertification as a certified lay minister ( )

1. What year did you first become certified as a lay minister? _____

2. Date of last review of CLM status: _____ Approved: _____ yes _____ no

3. What year did you complete your last approved continuing education event? _____

4. What was the title of your last approved continuing education event? _____

(Upon completion of an approved continuing education event and ministry review by his/her church council or charge conference WHERE MEMBERSHIP IS HELD, or if under assignment WHERE ASSIGNED, the CLM requests a letter of recommendation from his/her district superintendent. The CLM candidate then applies in writing and appears before the district committee on ordained ministry for interview and recommendation for recertification.)

(Part 3) REQUEST OF THE CERTIFIED LAY MINISTER

I request a recommendation from my pastor and church council or charge conference to become a certified lay minister.

Date _____ Certified Lay Servant _____

For those not currently under assignment:

( ) I request a ministry review by my church council/charge conference where my membership is held. *(every two years)*

For those currently under assignment:

( ) I request a ministry review by the church council/charge conference where I am assigned. *(every two years)*

Date _____ Certified Lay Minister _____

(Part 4) RECOMMENDATION OF THE PASTOR (for initial application)

I recommend concurrence with the request of this person to become or continue as a certified lay minister.

Date _____ Pastor _____

(Part 5) RECOMMENDATION OF THE CHURCH COUNCIL/CHARGE CONFERENCE

The church council or charge conference of _____ (church/charge) recommends the above

person become or continue as a certified lay minister.

Date _____ Church Council Chair _____

(Part 6) MINISTRIES OF THE CERTIFIED LAY MINISTER

During the past year, I have participated in *caring ministries* as follows:

_____ served as a volunteer in a caregiving institution

_____ provided one-on-one caring

_____ at a hospital, nursing home, or to a shut-in

_____ in membership/evangelism visitation

_____ served in caring/outreach projects (food pantry, prison ministry, etc.)

_____ other caring activities (Please list) _____

During the past year, I have participated in *leading ministries* as follows:

_____ served as member of committee, board, commission, council, task force, etc.

_____ served as a volunteer at a community agency

_____ served at my local church

_____ served beyond my local church

_____ served on my district _____ conference _____ jurisdiction _____ general church level

_____ other leading activities (Please list) _____

During the past year, I have participated in *communicating ministries* as follows:

_____ brought message in _____ worship services

_____ served as worship leader in _____ services

_____ delivered _____ devotional messages

_____ taught _____ classes

_____ shared my faith story _____

_____ other speaking activities (Please list) _____

During the past year, I have participated in additional opportunities for ministry as follows:

_____

(Part 7) PERSONAL AND SPIRITUAL GROWTH BY THE CERTIFIED LAY MINISTER

In what activities have you engaged and/or what books have you read or used during the past year to help you develop your devotional life; improve your understanding of the Bible; improve your understanding of The United Methodist Church; and improve your skills in caring, leading, communicating, and speaking?

_____

(Part 8) FEEDBACK BY THE CERTIFIED LAY MINISTER

Do you feel called to be in service in any area of ministry, either in the church or outside the church, in which you are not currently involved? _____ yes _____ no. If yes, please list those areas below: _____

(Revised December 2016)

LAY SERVANT/SPEAKER/MINISTER RECORD

Name _____

Address _____

City/State/Zip _____

Home Phone _____ Work Phone _____

Local Church _____ District _____

BASIC COURSE COMPLETED: (Date and District/Other)

_____

Approved as:

Certified Lay Servant _____
(Date)

Certified Lay Speaker _____
(Date)

District Committee on Lay Servant Ministries Interview _____
(Date)

Conference Committee Approval _____
(Date)

Certified Lay Minister _____
(Date)

District Committee on Ordained Ministries Interview _____
(Date)

Conference Committee Approval _____
(Date)

ADVANCED COURSES COMPLETED:

Title	Date	Yearly Report Received	Date Certified/ Recertified

Follow-up contacts: _____

LAY SERVANT MINISTRIES TRAINING CHECKLIST

(This form is also available at www.umcdiscipleship.org/laity under Lay Servant Ministries Resources.)

TWELVE TO TWENTY-FOUR MONTHS BEFORE

❑ Convene the committee on lay servant ministries and make plans for the training events for the next twelve to eighteen months. Set the tentative dates and sites. (Note: At convening, the committee will also perform the SIX-MONTHS and THREE-MONTHS BEFORE tasks below.)

❑ Estimate the budget needs for the training events planned and forward those to the agency responsible for funding lay servant training. (See paragraph on "Funding.")

SIX MONTHS BEFORE

❑ Meet with the committee to choose/finalize site and dates and consider possible courses and leaders.

❑ Reconfirm dates on calendars of the conference and district. Look for conflicts on community and local school calendars.

❑ Invite leaders to participate.

❑ When information is finalized, place event(s) on conference and district web calendars.

❑ Reserve site for the course by written or e-mail request and with return confirmation.

❑ Ask current lay servants, district superintendents, and pastors to suggest people who might be interested in receiving the training.

❑ Prepare the registration form. Consider meals (menu or service by the hosting church). If an e-book version is available, the option should be provided on the form.

❑ E-mail lay servants, asking them to enroll in the advanced or refresher course.

❑ Establish date and place for a consecration service and invite the bishop and district superintendents to participate.

❑ If desired, arrange through the conference office or through a nearby college the granting of continuing education units (CEUs) for courses.

THREE MONTHS BEFORE

❑ Convene the committee with the course leaders to check plans and answer questions for one another.

❑ Write a news story about the upcoming training. (Include a photo taken during the last school or a photo of a lay servant in ministry. It will make your story more appealing.)

❑ Prepare a one-page flyer (with a registration form included) about the event. Attach it to e-mails to pastors, churches, lay servants. Send it to other district directors. Link it to the web calendar item. Mail it to those without e-mail.

❑ Send a short e-mail notice about the upcoming training to key leaders and pastors in your district; ask them to include it in their church newsletters or post it on a bulletin board.

❑ Order or prepare forms to collect information needed to grant CEUs. (Some institutions will supply preprinted forms, but you will still need to arrange to have them sent to you.)

❑ If a consecration service is to be held as a separate event for the district, decide as a committee on a time and place and who will plan the event.

❑ Order texts, certificates, or other materials you wish to have available at the school and the consecration service.

SIX WEEKS BEFORE

❑ Check with leaders to find out what audiovisual equipment they will need. Reserve equipment.

❑ Verify that books and other materials have arrived and that the registrar is sending the books to those registering.

❑ Verify that CEU forms are ready for participants to complete.

❑ Reconfirm reservations for the rooms you will be using.

❑ Arrange for payment of leaders, if necessary.

❑ Arrange for payment for use of the site, if necessary.

❑ Send a press release about your training to your local paper. Include information on lay servant ministries and note that lay servants are available to speak on various moral or religious topics. Include contact information.

ONE TO TWO WEEKS BEFORE

❑ Check on book availability. Order more if needed.

❑ Determine what time the building will be open to set up for the training. Get contact information to call in case the building is not open when you arrive or in case of problems.

❑ Check with leaders regarding their last-minute needs.

❑ Assemble resources by the session in which they will be used and label them. Get large nametags for participants and leaders. Make direction signs for rooms.

❑ Complete a listing of those preregistered to provide leaders with a preliminary count.

❑ Assemble pens, paper, forms, and handouts according to the sessions in which they will be needed.

❑ Assemble audiovisual equipment requested by the instructors, and check to be sure that it works properly.

❑ Make arrangements for hospitality and refreshments.

ON EACH TRAINING DAY

❑ Arrive at least one hour before the event is scheduled to begin. Check the sound system (if one is used) and all audiovisual equipment.

❑ Assemble texts, registration table, registration materials, and nametags for easy distribution.

❑ Arrange chairs and worktables to encourage conversation among candidates.

❑ Have all of your "busy" work done early, so that you can spend time welcoming the participants.

❑ Make yourself available to the participants during the break and after the session for one-on-one conversations that might be requested or required.

ONE WEEK AFTER TRAINING ENDS

❑ Write short thank-you notes to the bishop, district superintendents, leaders, and committee members who participated. Pay stipends or facility rent as required.

❑ E-mail a roster of the participants to other directors and to the pastors of each participant informing him or her of the participant's successful completion of the course.

❑ Write a thank-you note to the host site.

AS SOON AS POSSIBLE AFTER EVENT

❑ Reconvene the committee to discuss the evaluations.

❑ Give leaders a summary of the evaluations by participants so that they can learn how to strengthen their leadership.

❑ Update committee records for participants.

❑ Hold a consecration service, awarding certificates and recognizing new and continuing certified lay servants.

LAY SERVANT MINISTRIES COURSE FEEDBACK FORM

Course Title: _____

Leader's Name: _____

Facilities   Poor—Excellent

Size of room 1 2 3 4 5

Lighting 1 2 3 4 5

Ease of hearing 1 2 3 4 5

Table space 1 2 3 4 5

Chairs 1 2 3 4 5

Overall location 1 2 3 4 5

Comments:

_____

_____

Leader   Poor—Excellent

Preparation 1 2 3 4 5

Eye contact with class 1 2 3 4 5

Understanding of students'
needs, goals, knowledge 1 2 3 4 5

Use of examples, stories 1 2 3 4 5

Use of facts, statistics 1 2 3 4 5

Use of humor 1 2 3 4 5

Use of audiovisuals 1 2 3 4 5

Use of inclusive language 1 2 3 4 5

Speed of speaking 1 2 3 4 5

Use of information given by
students during discussion 1 2 3 4 5

Response to student
questions 1 2 3 4 5

Suggestions for applying
course content 1 2 3 4 5

Comments:

_____

_____

Content   Poor—Excellent

Usefulness 1 2 3 4 5

Clarity of presentation 1 2 3 4 5

Sufficient detail 1 2 3 4 5

Parts clearly linked to
one another 1 2 3 4 5

Sufficient time for
student presentations 1 2 3 4 5

Sufficient time for small-
group work 1 2 3 4 5

Comments:

_____

_____

Name of Participant (optional)

Date _____

Location of Course: _____

Date Course Began: _____

General:

1. What was the most helpful aspect of this course?

_____

_____

_____

2. What was the least helpful aspect of this course?

_____

_____

_____

3. How could publicity about lay servant ministries and training be more effective?

_____

_____

_____

4. Why did you sign up for this course?

_____

_____

_____

5. What should we do differently next time to make the course more helpful and effective?

_____

_____

_____

6. Who might be interested in the course the next time it is offered? (Include mailing address, if possible.)

_____

_____

PRESENTATION FEEDBACK FORM

PARTICIPANT NAME:

_____

PRESENTATION SUBJECT:

_____

_____

                                Needs Work—Bravo!

Eye contact with audience......................... 1 2 3 4 5

Use of Bible 1 2 3 4 5

Use of humor... 1 2 3 4 5

Use of examples 1 2 3 4 5

Use of clear, simple words........................ 1 2 3 4 5

Use of gestures 1 2 3 4 5

Use of notes 1 2 3 4 5

Speed of speaking.................................... 1 2 3 4 5

Logical progression of ideas...................... 1 2 3 4 5

Topic narrowed to fit time....................... 1 2 3 4 5

Sincerity.. 1 2 3 4 5

Hopefulness 1 2 3 4 5

Additional Comments _____

_____

_____

_____

_____

_____

_____

_____

_____

_____

_____

_____

Instructor_____   Date_____

CONGREGATIONAL EVALUATION OF A LAY SPEAKER

We prayerfully request your comments concerning the sermon delivered by one of our district's certified lay speakers. Your comments will aid in training and maintaining quality speakers. Your identity will be kept confidential.

Name of lay speaker: _____ Date of service: _____

Was the sermon well developed and delivered?

Other comments:

Would you recommend this lay speaker? _____ Yes _____ No

Name of church: _____

Address of church: _____

Your name: _____

Your position in the church: _____

Please send this form to: _____

District Director of Lay Servant Ministries: _____

LAY SERVANT MINISTRIES CERTIFIED LAY SERVANT FLOW CHART

Step 1: Have you completed "Introduction to Lay Ministry: The BASIC Course" and an advanced lay servant ministries course?

Answer: Yes	Action: • Submit application for certification as a certified lay servant. • Obtain recommendation from pastor and church council or charge conference.	Answer: No	Action: Not considered for certification as a lay servant

Step 2: Have you submitted an application for certification as a lay servant to the district committee on lay servant ministries or an equivalent structure (See ¶668.3)?

Answer: Yes	Action: District committee reviews qualifications for certification as a lay servant.	Answer: No	Action: Not certified as a lay servant

Step 3: Has the district committee on LSM approved your certification as a lay servant?

Answer: Yes	Action: Await certification from district committee on LSM.	Answer: No	Action: Not certified as a lay servant

Step 4: Have you completed requirements for recertification as a lay servant (submitted annual report and renewal application, obtained pastor and church council or charge conference recommendation, and completed at least one advanced LSM course every three years)?

Answer: Yes	Action: Await approval and recertification by the district committee on LSM.	Answer: No	Action: Not considered for recertification as a lay servant

LAY SERVANT MINISTRIES CERTIFIED LAY SPEAKER TRACK FLOW CHART

Step 1: Has the certified lay servant been recommended for the certified lay speaker track by pastor and church council or charge conference?

Decision: Yes	Result: Enter certified lay speaker track.	Decision: No	Result: Not considered for certification as a lay speaker; remain certified lay servant.

Step 2: Has the certified lay servant completed required courses for the lay speaker track (leading prayer, leading worship, discovering spiritual gifts, preaching, United Methodist heritage, and United Methodist polity)?

Decision: Yes	Result: Interview with district committee on LSM.	Decision: No	Result: Not considered for certification as a lay speaker; remain certified lay servant.

Step 3: Has the district committee on LSM recommended certification as a lay speaker?

Decision: Yes	Result: Await certification from the conference committee on LSM.	Decision: No	Result: Not considered for certification as a lay speaker; remain certified lay servant.

Step 4: Has the certified lay servant been approved by conference committee on LSM as a certified lay speaker?

Decision: Yes	Result:	Decision: No	Result: Not considered for lay speaker role; remain certified lay servant.
	• Certified as a lay speaker for pulpit supply. • Submit annual renewal application/report as a certified lay servant. • Complete an advanced LSM course at least once every 3 years. • For recertification as a lay speaker, go before the district committee on LSM for interview and recommendation to the conference committee on LSM every 3 years.		

LAY SERVANT MINISTRIES CERTIFIED LAY MINISTER TRACK FLOW CHART

Step 1: Is the certified lay servant recommended for the certified lay minister track by the pastor, church council or charge conference, and district superintendent?

Decision: Yes	Result: Enter certified lay minister track.	Decision: No	Result: Not considered for certification as a lay minister; remain certified lay servant.

Step 2: Has the certified lay servant completed required courses for the lay minister track (CLM Modules I–IV, or their equivalent)?

Decision: Yes	Result: Interview with district committee on ordained ministry.	Decision: No	Result: Not considered for certification as a lay minister; remain certified lay servant.

Step 3: Does the district committee on ordained ministry recommend certification as a lay minister?

Decision: Yes	Result: Await certification from the conference committee on LSM.	Decision: No	Result: Not considered for certification as a lay minister; remain certified lay servant.

Step 4: Approved by conference committee on LSM as a certified lay minister

Decision: Yes	Result: • Certified as a lay minister. • Submit annual renewal application/report as for a certified lay servant. • Complete an advanced LSM course or 10 hours of continuing education at least once every 2 years. • For recertification as a lay minister, go before district committee on ordained ministry for interview and recommendation to conference committee on LSM every 3 years.	Decision: No	Result: Not considered for lay minister role; remain certified lay servant.

USING THE APPRECIATIVE INQUIRY PROCESS TO ASSESS/PLAN YOUR WORK

(These forms are also available at www.umcdiscipleship.org/laity under Lay Servant Ministries Resources)

CONFERENCE DIRECTORS

Responsibilities	Appreciative Inquiry Assessment
Support the laity (lay servants and others) in spiritual formation and development of skills in leading, caring, communicating, and discipleship to help develop vital congregations and increase our missional presence in the community.	What is working well? _____ _____ How can it work better? _____ _____ What resources are available to help achieve success? _____ _____
Train district directors of LSM in their roles.	What is working well? _____ _____ How can it work better? _____ _____ What resources are available to help achieve success? _____ _____
Interpret the needs of the annual conference for training opportunities.	What is working well? _____ _____ How can it work better? _____ _____ What resources are available to help achieve success? _____ _____

Responsibilities	Appreciative Inquiry Assessment
Recruit qualified district directors who are certified lay servants.	What is working well? How can it work better? What resources are available to help achieve success?
Support district directors as they provide training opportunities for all laity.	What is working well? How can it work better? What resources are available to help achieve success?
Be alert to opportunities in which lay servants can serve and lead in mission.	What is working well? How can it work better? What resources are available to help achieve success?

Responsibilities	Appreciative Inquiry Assessment
Nurture and support lay servants in their various roles.	What is working well? How can it work better? What resources are available to help achieve success?

Keep accurate records of lay servants, lay speakers, and lay ministers within the conference and train district directors to do this within their districts.	**What is working well?** _____ _____ **How can it work better?** _____ _____ **What resources are available to help achieve success?** _____ _____
Provide for forms of recognition for lay servants, lay speakers, and lay ministers.	**What is working well?** _____ _____ **How can it work better?** _____ _____ **What resources are available to help achieve success?** _____ _____

Responsibilities	Appreciative Inquiry Assessment
Work to support the certified lay minister program where applicable.	**What is working well?** _____ _____ **How can it work better?** _____ _____ **What resources are available to help achieve success?** _____ _____
Chair the conference committee on lay servant ministries.	**What is working well?** _____ _____ **How can it work better?** _____ _____ **What resources are available to help achieve success?** _____ _____

USING THE APPRECIATIVE INQUIRY PROCESS TO ASSESS/PLAN YOUR WORK

(These forms are also available at www.umcdiscipleship.org/laity under Lay Servant Ministries Resources)

CONFERENCE COMMITTEE ON LAY SERVANT MINISTRIES

Responsibilities	Appreciative Inquiry Assessment
Set criteria and guidelines for district committees on lay servant ministries.	What is working well? How can it work better? What resources are available to help achieve success?
Using criteria established by Discipleship Ministries and the education committee of The Association of Conference Directors of Lay Servant Ministries: a) develop courses to fill a specific need within the annual conference, if not available through Discipleship Ministries. b) approve courses developed by district committees. c) approve alternative advanced courses (including online courses that meet the criteria for a lay servant ministries course).	What is working well? How can it work better? What resources are available to help achieve success?

Responsibilities	Appreciative Inquiry Assessment
Organize conference-wide lay servant ministries events.	What is working well? _____ _____ How can it work better? _____ _____ What resources are available to help achieve success? _____ _____
Cooperate with or partner with districts in conducting district events	What is working well? _____ _____ How can it work better? _____ _____ What resources are available to help achieve success? _____ _____
Train district directors to keep accurate records within their districts.	What is working well? _____ _____ How can it work better? _____ _____ What resources are available to help achieve success? _____ _____

Responsibilities	Appreciative Inquiry Assessment
Approve the recommendations for certification of lay speakers and lay ministers by their respective district committees.	What is working well? _____ _____ How can it work better? _____ _____ What resources are available to help achieve success? _____ _____

USING THE APPRECIATIVE INQUIRY PROCESS TO ASSESS/PLAN YOUR WORK

(These forms are also available at www.umcdiscipleship.org/laity; Lay Servant Ministries Resources)

DISTRICT DIRECTOR

Responsibilities	Appreciative Inquiry Assessment
Commit to support the laity (lay servants and others) in spiritual formation and development of skills in leading, caring, and communicating and discipleship to help develop vital congregations and increase our missional presence in the community.	What is working well? _____ _____ How can it work better? _____ _____ What resources are available to help achieve success? _____ _____
Interpret the needs of the district for training opportunities.	What is working well? _____ _____ How can it work better? _____ _____ What resources are available to help achieve success? _____ _____
Provide lay servant ministry course instructor training.	What is working well? _____ _____ How can it work better? _____ _____ What resources are available to help achieve success? _____ _____

Responsibilities	Appreciative Inquiry Assessment
Be alert to opportunities in which lay servants can serve.	What is working well? How can it work better? What resources are available to help achieve success?
Keep accurate records of lay servants within the district and help local church leaders to do this within their congregations.	What is working well? How can it work better? What resources are available to help achieve success?
Provide for forms of recognition for lay servants, lay speakers, and lay ministers.	What is working well? How can it work better? What resources are available to help achieve success?

Responsibilities	Appreciative Inquiry Assessment
Work to support the certified lay minister program where applicable.	What is working well? How can it work better? What resources are available to help achieve success?

Chair the district committee on lay servant ministries.	What is working well?
	How can it work better?
	What resources are available to help achieve success?

USING THE APPRECIATIVE INQUIRY PROCESS TO ASSESS/PLAN YOUR WORK

(These forms are also available at www.umcdiscipleship.org/laity under Lay Servant Ministries Resources)

DISTRICT COMMITTEE ON LAY SERVANT MINISTRIES

Responsibilities	Appreciative Inquiry Assessment
Plan and supervise the lay servant ministries program within the district.	What is working well? _____ _____ How can it work better? _____ _____ What resources are available to help achieve success? _____ _____
Provide basic and advanced training for lay servants as recommended by Discipleship Ministries and/or approved by the conference committee on lay servant ministries.	What is working well? _____ _____ How can it work better? _____ _____ What resources are available to help achieve success? _____ _____
Interview, review records, and recommend for approval by the conference committee on lay servant ministries certified lay servants who have completed requirements to be certified as lay speakers.	What is working well? _____ _____ How can it work better? _____ _____ What resources are available to help achieve success? _____ _____

Responsibilities	Appreciative Inquiry Assessment
Help match certified lay servants and lay speakers with service opportunities.	What is working well? _____ _____ How can it work better? _____ _____ What resources are available to help achieve success? _____ _____
Report to the pastor and church council/charge conference of each certified lay servant the courses that have been satisfactorily completed by certified lay servants and certified lay speakers.	What is working well? _____ _____ How can it work better? _____ _____ What resources are available to help achieve success? _____ _____
Plan advanced courses for lay servants that will enable certified lay servants, certified lay speakers, and certified lay ministers to maintain that recognition.	What is working well? _____ _____ How can it work better? _____ _____ What resources are available to help achieve success? _____ _____

GET-ACQUAINTED ACTIVITY

(Print this activity and have a copy for each participant distributed on the tables. May also be downloaded from www.umc-discipleship.org/laity under Lay Servant Ministries Resources.)

Find something you have in common with another person.

Find something unique about yourself and about that person.

Who has the most children?

Who has been at his or her employment the longest?

Who has the most family members living within 50 miles of the home?

Who has the longest middle name?

What is the most creative reason for liking or not liking that middle name?

Who has the most unusual pet?

GROUP DYNAMICS WORKSHEET

You will observe the teaching simulation. Look for these things and take notes to remember what you have observed.

What was the flow of the discussion? Did the teacher respond to or control everything as a gatekeeper, or did the discussion flow among the participants with occasional intervention of the teacher?

How were the various personalities managed (cared for, acknowledged, directed)? What was done about participants who were either very talkative or very shy?

Did any kind of teachable moment arise? If so, how did the teacher deal with it?

Did anyone besides the teacher emerge as a natural leader? What effect did that have on the group?

Did you observe an 'agenda' (hidden or otherwise) from any of the group members? If so, how did the teacher and/or group members deal with that?

What sort of tactics were used by anyone to derail the discussion? to bring it back to focus?

How well did the teacher include everyone who wanted to take part? How was that done?

What seemed to be the most important thing? the lesson? the people? the learning taking place? something else?

Overall, what did you see that will help you with the dynamics of a group?

GROUP DYNAMICS ROLES

Print out and cut this page into strips to give the volunteers their roles.

TEACHER

Since you will not have prepared a real lesson, choose a topic or Scripture that is familiar to you. You start the class and keep the conversation going. You will monitor the class dynamics to ensure that those who want to participate can do so and that those who derail the group somehow are contained (as politely as possible). You should be sensitive to the 'teachable moment' and open to the input and creativity of the group members.

HYPERACTIVE

You're having a hard time sitting still and constraining yourself. You can doodle or fidget or get up—something that indicates you have trouble focusing for very long. This is a simulation, so be realistic, but don't be obnoxious!

SHY

You can decide when and if to participate. Your shyness may be sufficient reason to just listen, but you should attempt to participate actively at least once.

FREQUENT TALKER

You LOVE to hear yourself talk, even if you aren't really saying anything. If the teacher attempts to contain you, you should listen, or at least appear to listen, for a while.

BUNNY TRAIL

You apparently have an interest in the side issues that can come up in a discussion. You're not all that keyed in to the main subject but are more than ready to go off on some tangent. You may be the one in the group who has some urgent need, secondary to the lesson, which becomes an occasion for the teachable moment.

FOCUSER

You are the one who likes to keep on track. If the discussion derails, you will find a way to focus on the main thing, including something that comes up that wasn't the main thing to begin with, but seems to need to be.

SYNTHESIZER

You like to bring all the threads of the discussion into some sort of order, if you can. That might mean listening until you are ready to bring the main points together, though you are free to participate at will.

TRAINING THE TRAINERS COURSE ANALYSIS WORKSHEET

1. What are the intelligences used?
2. What learning hooks do you see?
3. Over all, are all the intelligences represented with some balance? What is overused? underused?
4. If you were to adapt a session to make it more creative or appealing to a broader range of learning preferences, what might you do?

SESSION 1:

SESSION 2:

SESSION 3:

SESSION 4:

SESSION 5:

SUGGESTED CHANGES OR ADAPTATIONS (WHAT IS ADDED OR CHANGED? WHY?)

CPSIA information can be obtained
at www.ICGtesting.com
Printed in the USA
BVHW010524291218
536649BV00002B/2/P